GUITAR PEDALS

MASTERING**GUITAR**EFFECTS

Discover How to Use Pedals and Chain Effects to Get the Ultimate Guitar Tone

ROB**THORPE**

FUNDAMENTAL**CHANGES**

Guitar Pedals: Exploring Guitar Effects

Discover How to Use Pedals and Chain Effects to Get the Ultimate Guitar Tone

ISBN: 978-1-78933-039-7

Published by **www.fundamental-changes.com**

www.fundamental-changes.com

Twitter: **@robthorpemusic**

Over 10,000 fans on Facebook: **FundamentalChangesInGuitar**

Instagram: **FundamentalChanges**

For over 350 Free Guitar Lessons with Videos Check Out

www.fundamental-changes.com

Cover Image Copyright: Sofia Sourianou. Used by permission.

Audio recorded and mixed by Declan Pearson.

Contents

Introduction

How many legendary guitarists can be identified from just a single note? It's that unique combination of guitar, amp and pedals that has defined the signature sounds of the greats.

Guitar effects can enhance your playing with new dimensions of colour and texture. Often, the pedals you use become an integral part of the instrument, so in this book I'll help you understand how effects are used to broaden your tonal palette with style and authenticity.

Are you bedazzled by the variety of gadgets and doodads at your local guitar emporium? Do you look wistfully at your collection of pedals, frustrated that you aren't maximising their potential? Most guitarists are guilty of stockpiling guitar equipment. We are victims of chronic G.A.S. (Gear Acquisition Syndrome), so it's time to put your under-stomped effects pedals to work.

Your guitar tone can suggest a mood or genre just as effectively as any melody or chord progression. Adding a slow tremolo to chords can evoke the mood of a spy film. A shimmer of watery chorus and reverb can transform those same chords into an '80s pop song. Rocking on a wah-wah could even take those same chords into Motown territory.

Some effects are subtle, such as the tight compression that adds the "spank" to David Williams' parts on many of Michael Jackson's greatest hits. Other effects grab the limelight and transform a simple riff into an iconic hook, like the talk-box on Bon Jovi's *Livin' on a Prayer*.

More extreme and inventive use of effects can transform the guitar into something else entirely. For example, Tom Morello's use of whammy pedal in his "car alarm" solos with Rage Against the Machine. Delays and loopers extend the creative potential of effects pedals so that they become compositional tools that help the solo guitarist create otherwise impossible sonic tapestries.

Cunning use of pedals and effects enables the guitarist to transcend the limitations of range, polyphony and timbre inherent to the guitar.

In this book we will explore the most important effects available to guitarists. Each chapter is devoted to a different category. You'll learn what the controls do and hear stylistic musical examples of how they can be used in a range of settings.

After examining each effect type separately, we'll combine them in different ways to subtly change the sound, suggest essential pedals for different genres, and explore more complicated setups.

Finally, three creative guitarists with interesting rigs will share insights into the creative needs that influenced their choices and how they developed their current setup.

Of course, there are no hard and fast rules as to how you should use effects – the best way to get a working knowledge of their possibilities is to explore them through experimentation. So plug in and have fun!

Rob.

Get the Audio

The audio files for this book are available to download for free from **www.fundamental-changes.com.** The link is in the top right-hand corner. Simply select this book title from the drop-down menu and follow the instructions to get the audio.

We recommend that you download the files directly to your computer, not to your tablet, and extract them there before adding them to your media library. You can then put them on your tablet, iPod or burn them to CD. On the download page there is a help PDF and we also provide technical support via the contact form.

For over 350 Free Guitar Lessons with Videos Check out:

www.fundamental-changes.com

Twitter: **@robthorpemusic @guitar_joseph**

Over 10,000 fans on Facebook: **FundamentalChangesInGuitar**

Instagram: **FundamentalChanges**

Tone Really is in the Fingers

The old adage that "tone is in the fingers" still stands. Before delving into the box of electronic magic tricks, I want to highlight this point as a kind of guitar-practice disclaimer!

While any good guitarist has developed their overall sound via their instrument, amplifier and effects, their tone is always built on the foundation of solid technique, touch, ear and fretboard knowledge. Joe Satriani still sounds like himself playing a cheap guitar through a practice amp, and I wouldn't sound like Derek Trucks, even if I picked up his SG and plugged into his Alessandro amp.

Equally, I'm not suggesting that you spend the earth on high-end equipment. There is great quality available via budget range guitar amps and effects. The real key is knowing how to properly tweak the parameters.

Meanwhile, keep all the aspects of your musicianship in balance. It's tempting to fixate on certain areas and neglect others, but spread your time evenly – treat your tone development equally alongside all the other ingredients you need to grow as a musician.

Chapter One: All to Gain –
Fuzz, Distortion, Overdrive and Boosts

Filth, grit, dirt, gain, meat, balls, sustain, fuzz, crunch or overdrive. There are plenty of names for how the guitar signal can be distorted. Distortion is the most common treatment of the basic clean sound. It is so ubiquitous that you might not think of it as an effect at all. Distortion provides the most striking contrast to the clean guitar tone and is often the first pedal guitarists buy.

The types of distortion will be covered in roughly chronological order, starting with the advent of amplifier overdrive in the '60s, through to modern high gain sounds.

As with most aspects of music, the trend for distortion has seen an increase in gain and saturation as our tastes have acclimatised to new extremes. What now sounds warm and "classic" was once cutting edge, so we can only imagine the impact it must have had on audiences at the time.

Two examples of early overdrive include Link Wray's track *Rumble* (released in 1958) and The Kinks' *You Really Got Me* (1964). Wray's instrumental track was banned in certain places for fear its' raucous sound and titular reference would incite gang violence. His proto-distortion was achieved by stabbing holes in his speaker cones with a pencil. Similarly, Dave Davies of The Kinks slashed his speaker-cones with a razorblade to achieve the effect.

While Davies' and Wray's approach may be in the spirit of rock n' roll, thankfully technology has moved on and we can get the same effect in much less destructive ways.

There are three main types of gain pedal: overdrive, distortion and clean boost. The first two compress the signal and reduce the dynamic range of your playing. The boost should retain the full dynamic range and raise the volume by a fixed amount without colouring the sound.

We'll start with the earliest type of distortion, known as fuzz.

The Gospel of Valves

Valve (tube) amplifiers are considered superior to transistor amps by many players. The idea that valve technology is the holy grail of tone is still so prevalent that many pedal manufacturers market valve-driven pedals, sometimes with questionable benefit.

Valves start to clip and compress the sound in a very smooth and pleasing way as the input signal increases beyond a certain threshold. This is often referred to as *warmth*. Early amps didn't have master volume controls after the preamp stage, so the only way to get an overdriven sound was to turn the amp's gain up to 10.

Maxing out a full Marshall stack doesn't make for happy neighbours, so modern amps all feature master volume controls in addition to the pre-amp stage. This means you can push (turn up) the preamp using the channel volume or gain setting, while keeping the overdriven output at a safe and socially-minded volume.

This feature gets you fairly close to the classic saturated and overdriven amp tone of Hendrix, Led Zeppelin and Cream, but the power stage – those much bigger valves in your amp – is still not getting pushed enough to damage your hearing. For this reason, it is much better to gig with a smaller valve combo than something too big for the venue.

While you gain rockstar points for standing in front of a monolithic wall of speaker cabs, a 10-watt combo with the volume turned up will have plenty of oomph for your average pub gig or small venue. Besides, it will deliver much more tonal joy than a 100w head with its volume at 0.5!

That said, very few high-gain amps are made in sub 50w sizes, so the option of a 5w amp isn't possible. For metal players, or if you're just determined to ignore my suggestion and play a large amp regardless, you should investigate *Power Attenuators* (aka load boxes). These absorb some of the power output from a cranked amp and deliver a controllable output to the speaker. You can then safely turn both preamp and master volume up to the excite the valves while keeping the volume manageable.

In 1962, Gibson released the Maestro FZ-1, the first commercially available fuzz pedal that was designed to emulate the kind of distortion previously caused by ripped speakers, excessive volume or destructive modifications. Other products soon followed, including the **Vox Tone Bender** and **Arbiter FuzzFace** which was used for examples 1a and 1b below.

Example 1a

Jimi Hendrix was one of the earliest users of the Fuzz Face which provided his main rhythm sound, as in the following example. At the time they were a significantly cheaper alternative (1/5 of the price of the Maestro), although early models were very inconsistent. The components would react to temperature changes and were often mismatched. Hendrix would buy several at a time and they would be rotated, sometimes mid-performance! His engineer, Roger Mayer, would take the Fuzz Faces apart and construct working versions from the best components.

Set the fuzz to about 8 and keep a loose 1/16th note strumming motion throughout the first three bars to get the right feel. A single-coil bridge pickup would help with this.

Example 1b

Another of the most widely used fuzz pedals is the **Electro-Harmonix Big Muff**. This is popular with everyone from David Gilmour to Dinosaur Jr., as well as rock bassists searching for a rich distorted bass tone like Cliff Burton and Chris Wolstenholme of Muse.

The Big Muff is capable of some serious filth, but retains the warm "woolly" characteristic of fuzz, rather than the saturation and lack of dynamic response of more modern distortions. This riff shows the pedal used on both rhythm and lead ideas. Use the guitar's volume control to soften the tone for the power chords, then roll it to full, select the bridge pickup and dig in with the pick for the bluesy lick at the end.

Example 1c

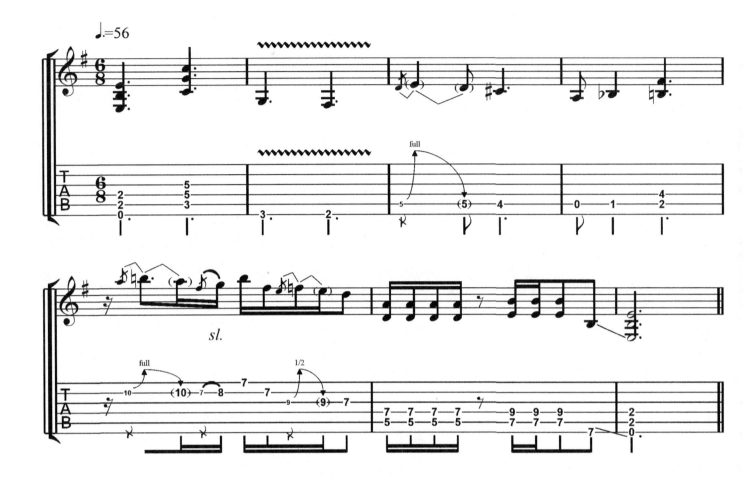

Boost pedals

A good booster pedal doesn't add distortion to the signal, but increases the guitar's signal level to drive your amp harder, so it produces more natural overdrive. A boost pedal can transform a clean sound into a crunchy semi-distorted tone without changing the amp settings. Or, if the amp is already distorted, the boost pedal can push a crunchy rhythm tone to a screaming lead sound.

The earliest boost effects appeared in the '60s and were focused on boosting the higher frequencies to give a bright treble-boost. You can hear the characteristically bright treble-booster sound on the earliest Clapton, Black Sabbath and Deep Purple recordings.

Boost pedals have myriad uses, though appear uncomplicated. Most should have only a single knob, marked "gain" or "level".

In the next example, we're using a clean boost to shake some life into the tube amp. The pedal used was a clone of the **Z-Vex Super Hard-On**.

Example 1d

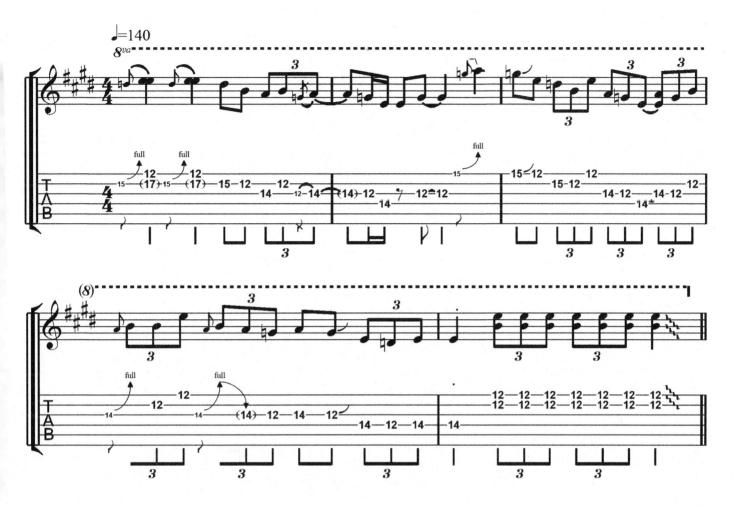

Another boost pedal is the long-serving **Ibanez Tubescreamer**, whose name describes its role perfectly. Introduced in the late '70s, the various incarnations of Tubescreamer have remained consistently popular with guitarists of all styles.

The Tubescreamer is a hybrid of a booster and overdrive pedal. It has a tone control alongside independent gain and level pots. Unlike traditional clean boosts, you can control the colouration of the sound and the level of its output volume.

This added flexibility means there are two main ways to use the effect.

The pedal has been set with moderate gain and a low level to provide its own overdrive without antagonising the amp. This lick is typical of blues-rock players like Stevie Ray Vaughan.

Example 1e

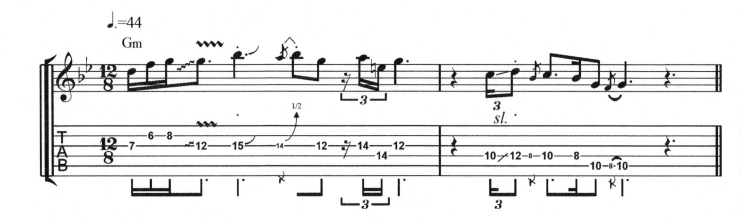

As the gain is raised we move towards an '80s rock rhythm tone à la Bryan Adams. From here, experiment by combining a boost pedal with other overdrives to appreciate how their gains interact.

Example 1f

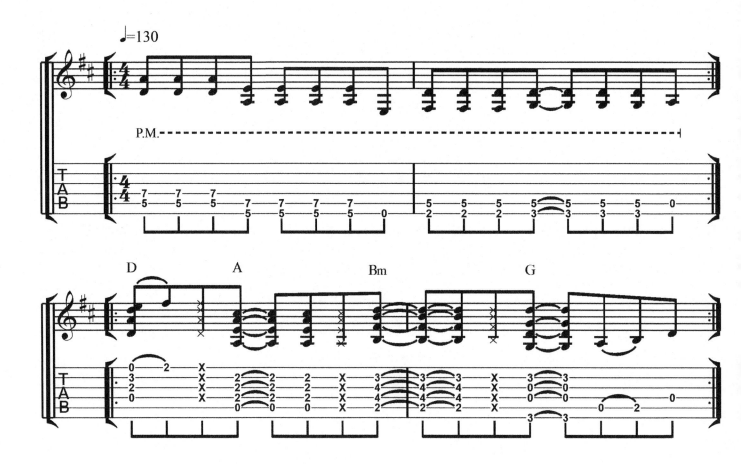

The final two examples cover the opposite approach. The pedal is set with a lower gain, but higher level, so that the pedal is providing a cleaner increase in the overall signal. The amplifier is being pushed harder by the input volume and produces a warm overdrive in response. Example 1g starts with a clean sound and then the pedal is engaged where notated for the lead fills.

This differs from Example 1d, because here the pedal is also providing its own colouration as well as boosting the signal level.

Example 1g

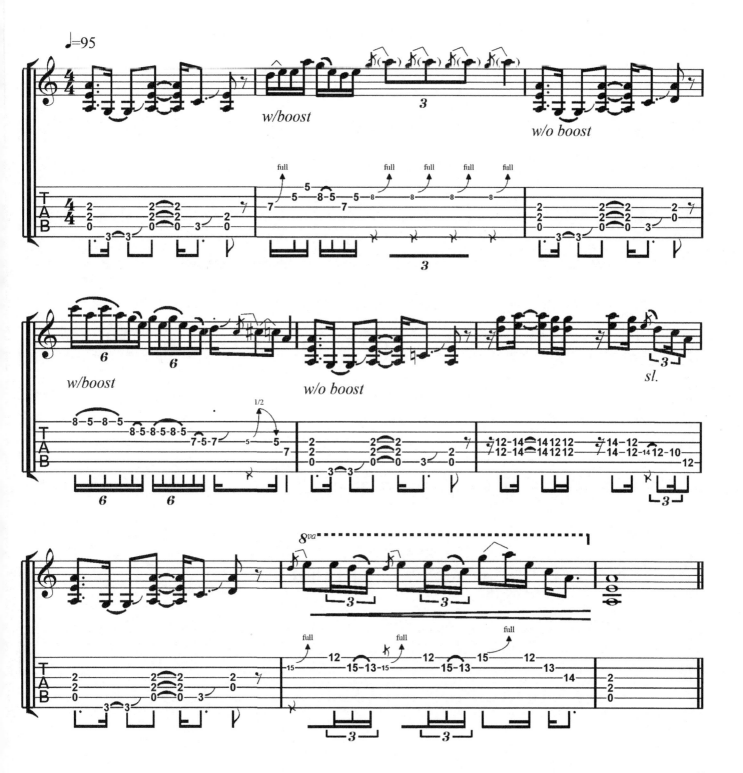

The same idea is now used in a metal context. This low gain/high volume setting is typical of a heavy metal players' approach to boost and overdrive pedals and the effect is used to colour an already distorted amp. Sequential gain stages (a combination of distortion pedals and amplifier) provide a more focused and controllable tone, rather than getting all the distortion from one source.

In Example 1h, the amp is already saturated enough for a metal rhythm tone, but the lower signal strength of the lead ideas needs boosting. Listen to the difference between the following rock solo played without, and then with, additional boost.

The amplifier used was a Mesa Boogie Dual Rectifier set to about 5 on the overdrive channel.

Example 1h

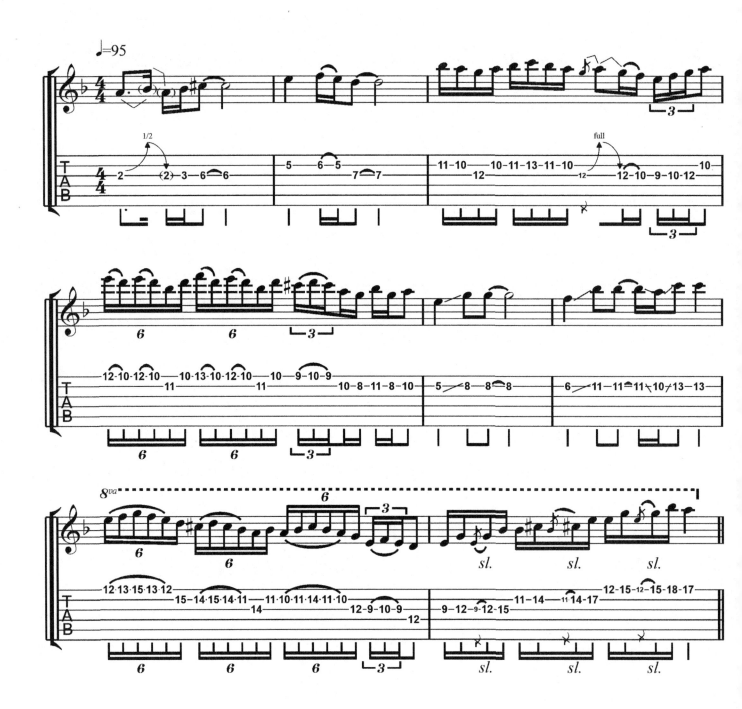

I often see students playing with too much gain to cover up poor technique and a lack of sustain. While the sustain from saturated distortion can be flattering, a compressor placed before moderate distortion would be better than piling on excessive gain.

Disputing the Middle Ground

The bass, middle and treble controls on your amp are a form of equalisation (EQ). EQ allows you to adjust the volume of individual *frequency bands*. Some amps, like Mesa Boogies, come with fine-tuneable graphic EQs, which divide the frequency range into even smaller divisions, such as 8-band, or 10-band-EQ. By comparison a standard bass/mid/treble setup is a 3-band EQ.

The typical classic rock tone *à la* Led Zeppelin is very mid-heavy with less bass and fewer high frequencies. By the early '80s heavy metal had diverged from hard rock and the guitar tones had become more abrasive to match the music. Marshall was still the amp manufacturer of choice, as it had been for Hendrix and Page. Metallica's first album *Kill 'em All* was recorded with a Marshall JCM 800 head, albeit modified by Jose Arrengando, whose wizardry also helped Van Halen achieve his signature "brown sound".

As metal songwriting got increasingly intricate and nuanced, the tonal requirements became more demanding in terms of precision and clarity. Two of the biggest bands to emerge in the early '90s featuring such technical playing were Pantera and Dream Theater. These found their hi-gain sound with solid-state Randall and Mesa Boogie Mark IIC+/Triaxis amps respectively.

Example 1i was recorded with a **Mesa Boogie Dual Rectifier** with the gain set to 6, and the middle frequencies set at 4 to provide a modest cut. A Tubescreamer was also placed in front of the amp to provide a small amount of additional gain.

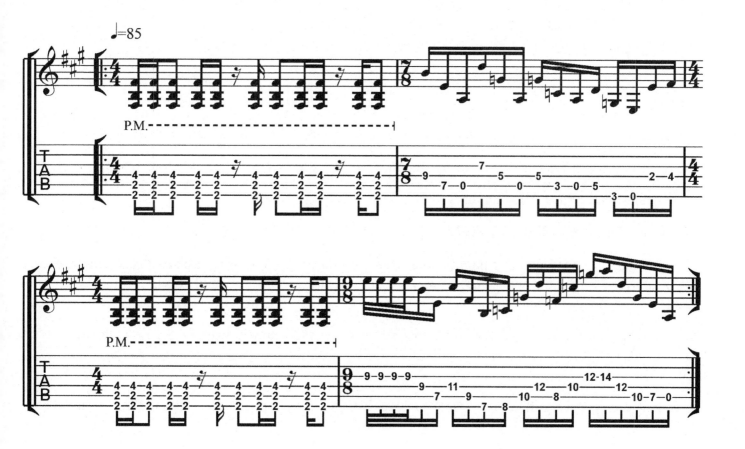

Since Nu-Metal and the more recent Djent subgenres made detuning much more widespread, the tonal requirement has shifted. 8-string guitars are tuned to F# as standard – nearly an octave lower than the 6th string E – making the respective frequency bands proportionally lower than in standard tuning.

It is easy for this tuning to become muddy and poorly defined, so the distortion is often set lower than you might think. When multi-tracking guitars in the studio, the gain can be much lower on each individual guitar, since the perceived level is cumulative.

The following example demonstrates this phenomenon by starting off with a single guitar then layering up three more identical performances. Each guitar is quite clean, but the end result certainly doesn't lack impact.

It was recorded on a 7-string guitar tuned down to G#. The effect was a **Reaper Pandemonium** – the John Brown signature overdrive based on the Fulltone OCD, but re-voiced specifically for this lower tuning.

Example 1j

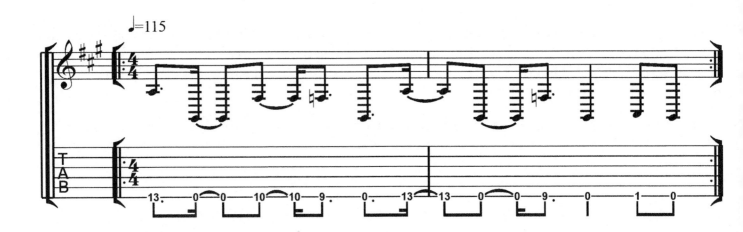

Distortion pedals are a "saturated" market (sorry!) and have expanded into countless varieties of products. The vast majority aim to replicate particularly revered amplifiers in a convenient pedal format, so to explore them would mean diving into the world of amplifiers, which is a subject worthy of its own weighty book.

The important points to consider if you are stepping into the world of pedals for the first time are:

a) the kind of tone you are looking for

b) what amplifier you will be playing through

A rock guitarist playing at home might be best served by a pedal replicating a classic large Marshall amp, while a player who has the opportunity to play with others at jams or gigs would benefit from a cleaner boost pedal and a quality small amplifier.

Keep in mind that it is the combination of your guitar, pedal and amp that matters. Wherever possible, try to test new pedals with your guitar and amplifier in the shop to avoid disappointment when you take a shiny new pedal home.

Of course, each pedal is different and you can never have too many options. Welcome to the slippery slope…

Recommended Listening for fuzz, distortion and overdrive tones:

John Mayall and the Bluesbreakers with Eric Clapton – *Hideaway* (Marshall '62 combo, Gibson Les Paul, and Dallas Rangemaster Treble Booster)

Jimi Hendrix – *Purple Haze* (Fuzz Face, Roger Mayer Octavia)

Gary Moore – *Out in the Fields* (Tubescreamer 808)

Nirvana – *Smells like Teen Spirit* (EH Big Muff)

Metallica – *Hit the Lights* (modded Marshall JCM800)

Pantera – *Cowboys from Hell* (Randall RG100ES)

Dream Theater – *On the Backs of Angels* (Mesa Boogie Mk. V)

Chapter Two: With or Without Echo: Delay

Delay effects cover a spectrum of technologies and stylistic applications, but here I'll focus on the most popular and recognisable uses of delay, finishing with a few lesser-spotted creative applications.

Analogue delays developed out of the experiments of *avantgarde* composers such as Pierre Schaffer and Karlheinz Stockhausen in the movement known as *musique concrète* (involving sounds assembled on tape before a performance, compared to live instrumental performance).

In the 1960s American composer Steve Reich also pioneered rhythmic compositions based on layering short tape loops in connection with the influential San Francisco Tape Music Centre.

These DIY musical experiments led to the development of purpose-built delay units using short sections of tape. Guitarist and inventor Les Paul built such a unit that became a hit with many country and rock 'n roll guitarists at the time, delivering the iconic "slap-back" sound associated with the genre.

Another pioneering device that has remained popular is the Echoplex. Built by Mike Battle in the late 1950s, this portable device allowed studio delay effects to be replicated live. It added the flexibility of control that we now recognise on all modern delay effects, such as feedback and the length of each repeat.

Let's start by understanding the separate parameters common to all delays. It is important (and great fun) to just experiment with your gear, discovering how it reacts through trial and error, but having a clear understanding of how each parameter functions will help you to predict how the pedal will react, and dial in specific effects.

Delay Time is the period between each repetition (or *tail*) and controls the length of the audio clip being repeated. If you alter the delay time while the effect is in use, you'll notice a change in pitch. On the original tape-based delays, the delay time would be controlled by the speed of the tape drive.

As the delay time gets longer the tape moves more slowly across the playback head. Lowering the speed while in operation makes the waveform appear to stretch, lowering the frequency and thus pitch. Modern digital delays replicate this behaviour in order to emulate their analogue predecessors.

Feedback refers to the number of repetitions of each delay sample. This too harks back to tape delays such as the Echoplex, where the output signal could be fed back into the input alongside the live guitar signal.

When only a fraction of the output is fed back, the delay repeats fade away naturally, but as feedback approaches 100% the device starts to over load and volume swells rapidly in much the same way as microphone or amplifier feedback. Once understood, delay feedback can be used to create interesting chaotic effects.

Mix balances the wet (effected) and dry (direct, unaffected) signals. This allows you to control how prominent the effect is. With the mix set to full, the direct guitar sound should be inaudible.

The first example is a typical rock lead guitar tone. Delay adds a sense of space and grandeur. The delay time is set to a long delay of 300ms (milliseconds). There are approximately three repeats and a low mix. This stops the delay cluttering the main guitar part too much during faster licks.

A prominent delay does mean mistakes or string noise come back to haunt you, so it's a great incentive to polish your technique.

Example 2a

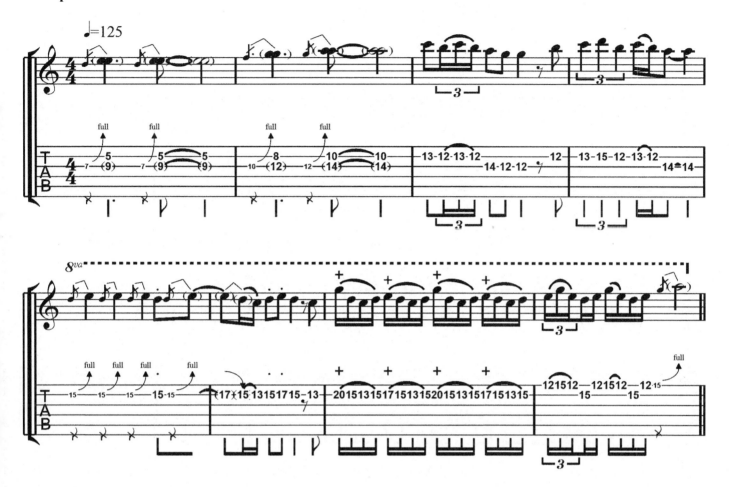

Next up is a rockabilly guitar passage featuring slap-back delay. This instantly recognisable delay setting is crucial to a convincing country guitar tone. Any classic country recording will illustrate this. Search for examples from Les Paul, Scotty Moore, Brian Setzer, or more recently Darrel Higham on Imelda May's recordings.

Dial in a short delay time for Example 2b with minimum feedback and a high mix. The goal here is a single repeat that is almost as loud as the original, occurring immediately after it. If you're playing a line of swung 1/8th notes the slap back delay should fit in between them. If the resulting sound seems too cluttered, experiment with lowering the mix level and shortening the delay time.

Example 2b

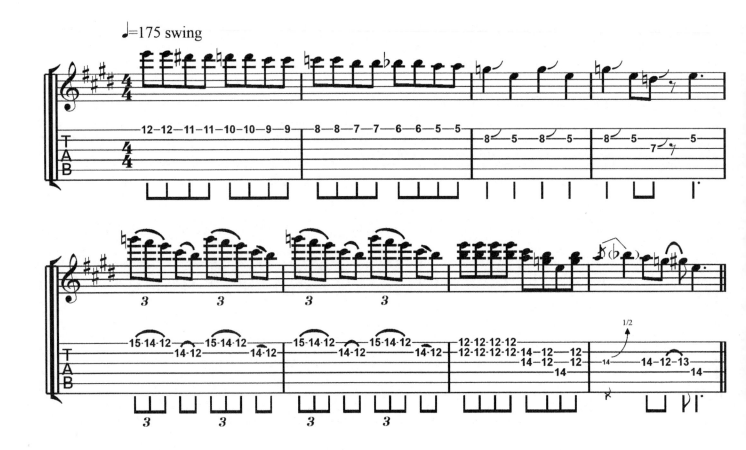

The third example features a medium delay time and a longer feedback setting. It is inspired by dub reggae – a style of reggae that developed out of studio engineering technology and the tradition of making remixes of existing tracks (the name being a reference to overdubbing audio).

The effect should be prominent in the mix, decaying gradually over several repeats. In dub reggae tracks, many layers of the music are treated with delay. Listen to some of the pioneers of dub, such as King Tubby, and Lee "Scratch" Perry, where the vocals, horns and drums are sometimes all effected. The Police embraced this production technique on the hi-hat cymbals in their classic *Walking on the Moon*.

Example 2c

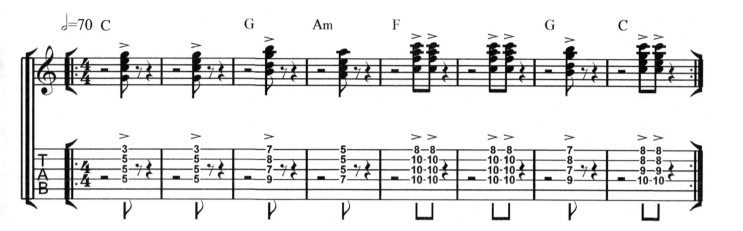

Synchronising to Tempo

So far, we haven't worried about the exact rate of delay. But, to achieve certain musical effects, the rhythm of the tails should be synchronised with the tempo of the song.

Most modern delays feature a built-in tap-tempo button, or the facility to connect an external one, but to explain what is going on behind the scenes I will work through the "old-fashioned" method.

If the delay is measured in milliseconds on your device, then first we need to know the BPM (beats-per-minute) of the song in question. This can be done by counting the number of beats played over the course of a minute (or fraction of a minute), or by using a metronome.

The BPM is then converted into the duration of each 1/4 note beat in milliseconds (1/1000th of a second)

$$(60/BPM) \times 1000 = \text{duration of a 1/4 note in } ms$$

Then decide on the rhythmic subdivision you wish the delay to "play". **Fig 2.1** represents other common rhythms as proportions of a beat. If the BPM is represented by a 1/4 note, then the table below represents the figure the BPM should be multiplied by in order to calculate the duration of each subdivision.

Fig. 2a

Rhythmic Subdivision	Proportion of 1/4 note pulse	Time multiplier	Example: ___ = 100 bpm (60/100)x1000=600 ms
♩ 1/2th /minim	Double	x 2	600 x 2 = 1200 ms
♪ 1/8th /quaver	1/2	x 0.5	600 x 0.5 = 300 ms
♪· dotted 1/8th	3/4	x 0.75	600 x 0.75 = 450 ms
♪³♪ swung 1/8th	2/3	x $0.66^{\dot{6}}$	600 x $0.6\dot{6}6$ = 400 ms
♪ 1/16th /semiquaver	1/4	x 0.25	600 x 0.25 = 150 ms

If your pedal doesn't have a digital time input or a tap tempo, you'll have to fine-tune the delay by ear. With the lowest possible feedback, play single notes in time with a metronome set to the desired tempo, then turn the delay-time control until the single repeat is also in time with the metronome's pulse.

This takes a good ear for rhythmic subdivision and timing, especially if you are trying to set a dotted 1/8th note by ear.

I've written the bpm for each musical example, but you'll have to do the rest.

In the following examples, the tablature contains only the notes you play, and the notes created by the delay effect are bracketed on the upper stave to help you picture how the complete part will sound.

The first synchronised delay example is a metal rhythm idea with a 1/2 note delay. There are a small number of repeats, and the level is set at about 50% so as not to clutter the main part.

I separated the effect output during recording, so that the delays are given a gated reverb and EQ while the direct signal is dry. Gated reverb provides a sense of sonic foreground and background (which will be discussed in the reverb chapter). Removing the lower frequencies with EQ means the note attacks are preserved without muddying the overall sound.

Example 2d

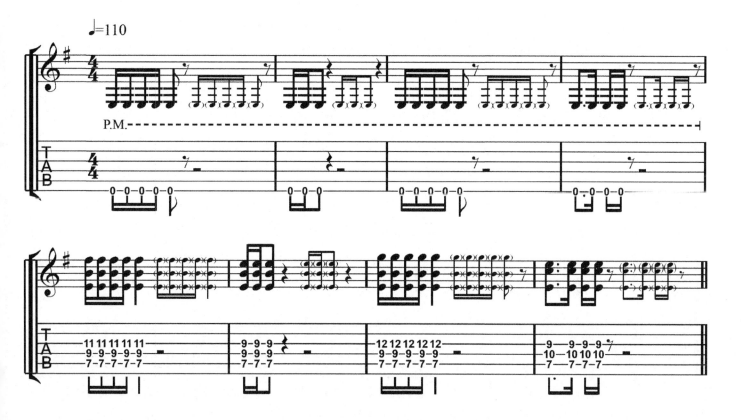

The following four examples feature much faster delays that dramatically alter the character of the part. The effect level is turned up to be balanced with the direct guitar sound, and the rigid timing of the notes produced by the effect gives them the feel of sequenced electronic music. So, pay attention in case you ever get called in for a disco gig…!

The first pattern is set to an 1/8th note delay (double the bpm). The live guitar plays staccato (short notes) on beat 1 of every bar. Turn the feedback control up until you're getting enough repeats to fill the gap. There should be seven notes with which to fill the remaining 1/8th note notes in the bar.

Example 2e

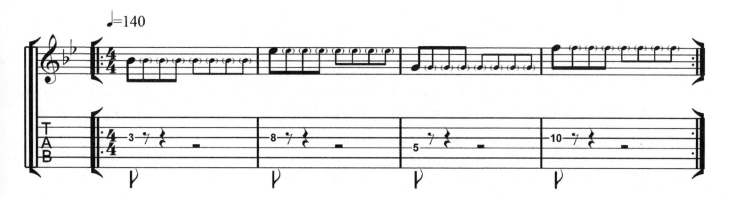

Next the feedback is set to zero to produce a single repeat, and we switch to a 1/16th note delay time (bpm x4). The live guitar part plays constant 1/8th notes, between which the delay will immediately duplicate each pitch to give the impression of a 1/16th note line.

Start by keeping the notes as short and punchy as possible by releasing the grip with your fretting hand. Towards the end of the example the music builds up; I allow the notes to ring slightly longer and the overlap adds to the intensity.

Make sure you can play the part evenly and in time before engaging the effect. It can be disorientating to keep playing your part accurately when there are extra notes coming out of your amp!

Disclaimer: though your practice woes may seem over, this trick is not an excuse for weak alternate picking!

Example 2f

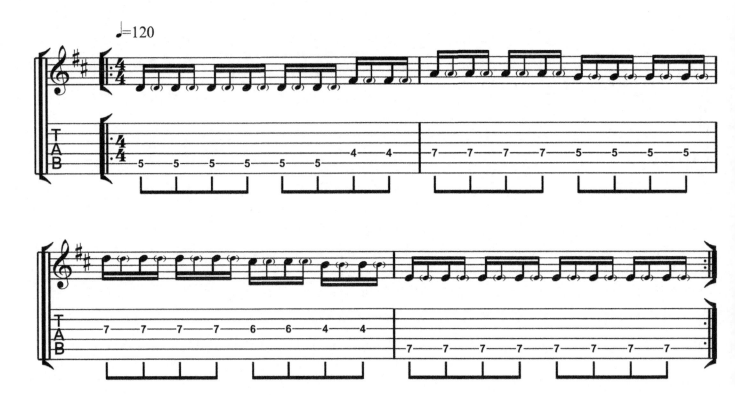

For the next two synchronised ideas, the delay time is extended to provide a dotted 1/8th note delay. This texture has been used by many players to produce impossibly fast melodic and arpeggio lines with the accuracy of a synthesizer and step-sequencer.

The dotted rhythm means the delay tail occurs three 1/16th notes after the played note. In a melodic guitar line this disguises the technique and blends the live and delayed notes seamlessly.

I've composed a simple chord progression, arpeggiating common shapes in a stream of 1/8th notes. They are also played slightly palm muted to give them more rhythmic definition.

It's especially important that these ideas are performed with the delay placed *after* the distortion so that the delay is copying the distorted guitar sound. If the delay was placed before, and notes were allowed to ring together, they would be overly distorted, making the texture messy and indistinct.

Example 2g

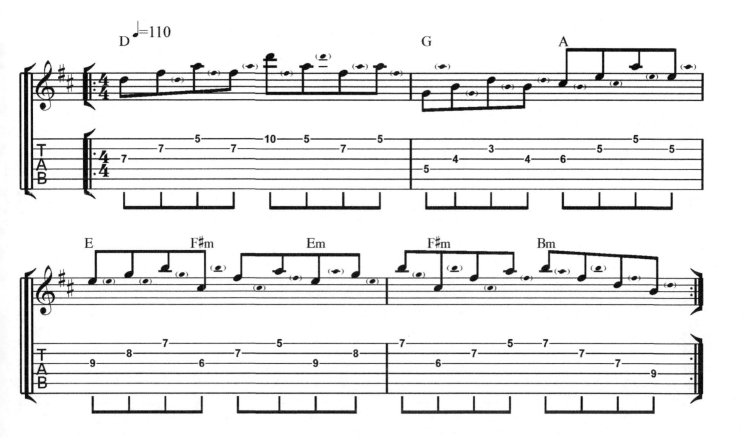

Here is a much faster version showing how this compositional technique can be used to provide a flowing texture. It would otherwise be impossible to achieve such smoothness and control over each note's articulation.

Example 2h

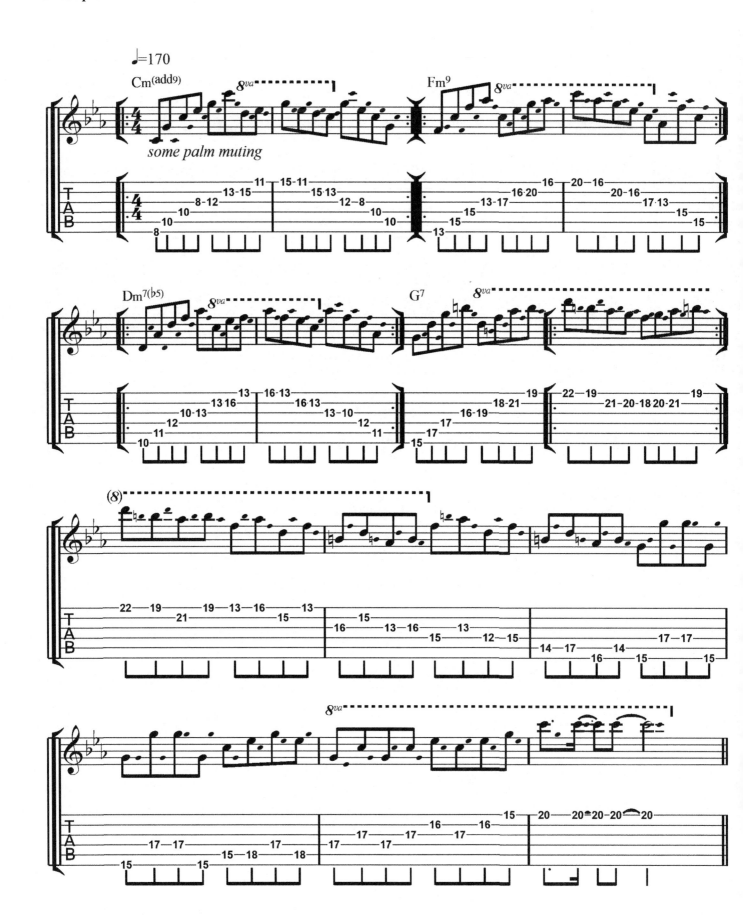

Just to turn the above idea on its head I've written a U2-inspired chordal part that features a 1/4 note delay, while the performed part's rhythm is in dotted 1/8th notes. The mix is lower to make the effect slightly less prominent.

Contrary to the previous examples, the effect has been placed *before* the lightly overdriven amp, which helps blur the sound together and provide a "cloud" of ringing chord tones.

Be careful with the syncopated rhythm of the played part. Hold the chord shapes down throughout and control the amount of ringing with a little palm muting.

The Edge often uses two synchronised delays in combination – one set to a 1/4 note and the second dotted 1/8th.

Example 2i

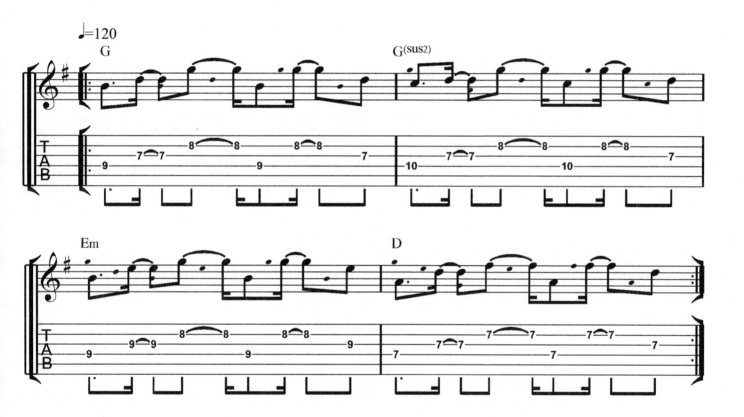

Before harmonisers were invented, several guitarists would use synchronised delays to produce a stack of guitar harmonies. Brian May is well known for tracking many layers of guitars in the studio with Queen, but in certain instances uses a pair of delays.

A prominent use of this method occurs at 4:00 minutes in *Brighton Rock* where you can clearly hear the right-panned guitar start one note after the left-panned one. The displacement produces some pleasing harmonies.

I'll discuss a little more theory behind producing consonant harmonies in the chapter on pitch-shifting.

The next two licks use two independent delay effects. One delay is set to a 1/4 note and the second is set to a 1/2 note. The first demonstrates the principle on a simple ascending E natural minor scale.

To make the effect more pronounced, the delays are panned hard left and right in the mix. Live, each could be sent to its own amplifier.

The notation shows how the delayed melodies create stacked harmonies of a 3rd and 5th above the root. The dry signal has moved up the scale by two steps by the time the first delay repeats, so that the interval of a 3rd occurs between the two parts. Both parts then ascend two more steps by the time the second delay enters with the starting note, to produce a full E minor triad.

Example 2j

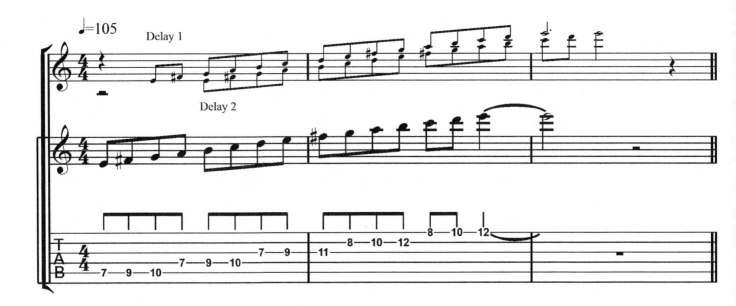

The second harmony lick uses the same principle with a more musical melody. The staggered entries of each melody give the impression of a classical fugue.

Much like a fugue, the example was composed by copying the first few notes on the second and third parts, then writing in the next phrase of the principle melody, so as to compliment the harmonies. This was then replicated in the second and third parts, before repeating the process for the following few notes.

If you are applying this effect without a metronome or backing track, give yourself a count-in by playing a single note and using the repeats to gauge the tempo.

Example 2k

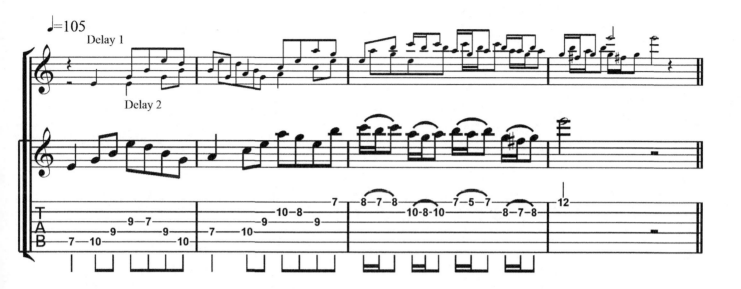

Reverse Guitar Solo Emulation

A reverse delay setting can be used like an ordinary delay to provide presence and space. Reversing the waveforms means each tail fades in gradually compared to the normal short attack, as illustrated in Figure 2b. For this reason, a reverse delay can provide a smoother texture.

Fig. 2b

Forward: short attack, long decay   Reversed: long attack, short decay

However, I want to demonstrate how the delay pedal can be used to replicate a "backwards guitar solo".

During the studio experiments of the '60s and '70s, when music was recorded onto tape, musicians often used tape manipulation techniques to alter their sound. Playing tape backwards to create strange otherworldly discombobulation became very popular! Listen to Hendrix's *Castles Made of Sand* and The Red Hot Chili Peppers' *Give It Away* to hear that instantly recognisable warped sound. Typically, Dream Theater managed to go one step beyond on their song *Misunderstood*, which features a reverse guitar solo, but played in harmony!

To start with, I composed a short guitar solo in the key of A minor. This is the melody I want the end result to sound like.

Example 2la – forward solo notation

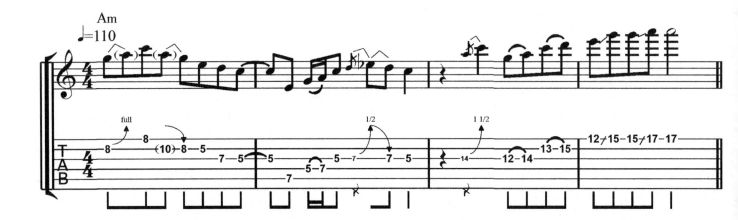

The second step is to *retrograde* or reverse the notation Thankfully, this is very easy to do with the advanced features of notation software.

I've included the audio of this twice: first as I performed it, then with the lead guitar audio reversed to sound like Example 2la.

Example 2lb – reversed solo notation

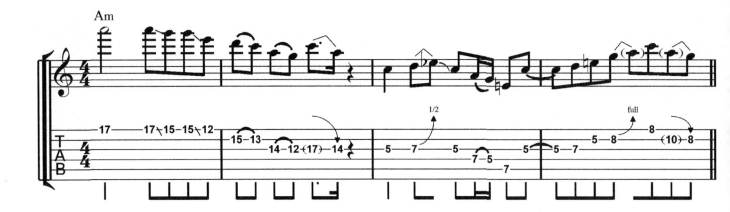

Finally, the reverse delay effect is used to reverse the "backwards" solo and produce an approximation of the studio trickery without resorting to bending the space-time continuum!

The delay pedal must be able to split the wet and dry sounds. Mute the direct guitar sound completely and select minimum feedback so that only one tail is produced.

For the most authentic results, Example 2lc moves the solo two beats ahead, so that the delay effect will be played approximately where the original melody was intended. This means you'll be playing ahead of the track, which at first can be quite disorientating.

Example 2lc – performance version

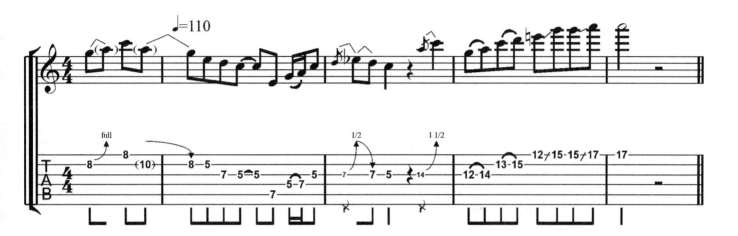

Complicated stuff! But if you have to reproduce any songs with reversed solos then this process captures the vibe convincingly.

The final example creates a sound similar to the resonance that occurs when microphones or guitars are on the edge of feeding back. Any tone gets a jarring tail after it, and some notes will resonate more than others. If you want to replicate this sound, then imitating it with a delay is less risky than setting your equipment up to feedback acoustically.

If you turn the feedback on the pedal up to full to create infinite repeats, the pedal starts to feedback uncontrollably and the output swells in volume. Roll back the feedback just far enough so that the sound dies after a second or two. Set the delay time to about 50ms, so the individual repeats aren't really audible.

For this eerie musical example, I picked close to the bridge to bring out the trebly sound and played an atonal melody to compliment the unhinged mood.

Example 2m

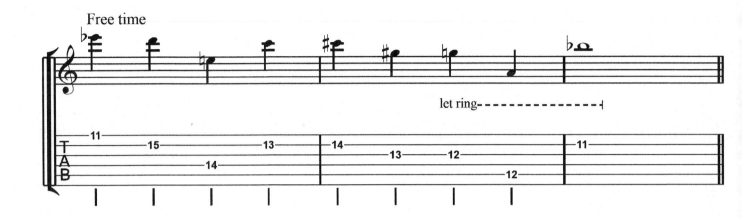

Recommended Listening for delay use:

Scotty Moore – *That's All Right*
Steve Vai – *Blue Powder*
U2 – *Beautiful Day*
King Tubby – *King of Zion Dub (feat. Barry Brown)*
The Police – *Walking on the Moon* (drum hi-hat cymbals)
Iron Maiden – *Wasted Years* (intro riff)
Queen – *Brighton Rock* (4:00)
The Beatles – *Tomorrow Never Knows* (reverse tape effects)
Metallica - *Blackened* (reversed intro section)

Dotted 1/8th delay:

Albert Lee – *Country Boy*
U2 – *Where the Streets Have No Name*
Dream Theater – *Surrounded*
Extreme – *Flight of the Wounded Bumblebee*
Nils Frahm – *An Aborted Beginning/Says*

Chapter Three: A Heavenly Chorus –
Modulation

Chorus, phaser, flanger and tremolo are collectively referred to as modulation effects. This family of effects control how waveforms interact when layered and modified. The sound each effect produces can easily be confused. Adjectives like spacious, watery or swirly are often applied to them, as their fluctuations of tone seem to shimmer like iridescent oil on water.

Phaser

The earliest effect of the group is the phaser, or phase-shifter. As with delays, phasers were born out of studio experimentation long before compact guitar pedals were produced. The pedal splits the dry signal and runs one channel through an all-pass filter, which inverts the *phase position* of chosen frequencies within the signal.

The phaser does not delay the audio signal, it just flips the position of the wave in its oscillation.

On its own, phase changes are imperceptible to human hearing. The consequence of the change is heard when the modulated path is mixed back in with the unmodulated path. Those frequencies which are now "out of phase" interact destructively to cut the overall amplitude. This produces a notch in the spectrum. The notch sweeps up and down the range of frequencies in the signal at a rate dictated by an LFO (Low Frequency Oscillator).

Phasers typically chain several filters together (known as stages), each acting on different frequencies. The more stages, the deeper and more complex the effect.

For all of these examples I used **KMA Machines**' brilliant 4-stage analogue phaser, disconcertingly christened **Astrospurt**. While capable of some berserk feedback effects, the Astrospurt is also a very practical classic phaser.

The most common controls on a phaser are:

RATE (the most common control of all). On **MXR**'s iconic **Phase 90**, it's the *only* control and affects the the speed of the sweeping effect. In technical terms, it controls the frequency of the low frequency oscillator (LFO) which drives the phaser's all-pass filter.

DEPTH controls how deep the notches in the frequency spectrum are. More of the out-of-phase signal is mixed in, so there is more destructive interference between the two. When the wet and dry are balanced 50:50, then the phasing will be strongest.

RESONANCE controls the amount of wet signal fed back into the phaser stages. The more signal is passed through the effect again, the more intense the contrast.

SHAPE/STEP is less common on compact pedals, but this changes the waveform of the LFO to make different sweep patterns. A step phaser uses a square wave which makes the notch move suddenly up and down the frequency spectrum, rather than sweeping smoothly.

Example 3a echoes David Gilmour's psychedelic chord playing in Pink Floyd. Phasers are particularly dramatic on clean tones. For this spacious arpeggiation, the phaser is set to modulate slowly with quite a lot of depth.

The original effect on *that* Shiny Diamond chord is created by a **Univibe** pedal, a subtly different '60s phaser popular with Hendrix, Robin Trower and David Gilmour, but the modern phaser provides us with a convincing substitute.

Example 3a

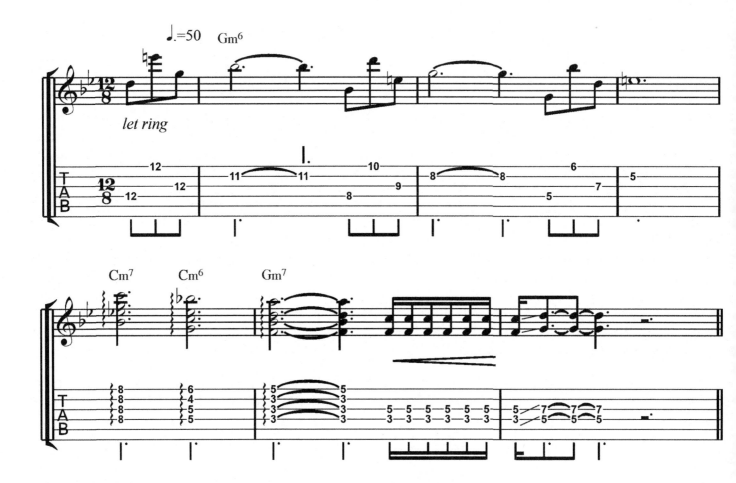

Next, we move from the '70s to the early '80s with a Van Halen inspired riff. Eddie Van Halen popularised the phaser pedal and is particularly associated with **MXR's Phase 90**. To nail this tone, use forceful hybrid picking to get a good percussive twang out of the strings.

The four-bar intro section features a flanger with a very slow rate to illustrate another of Van Halen's famous textures.

Example 3b

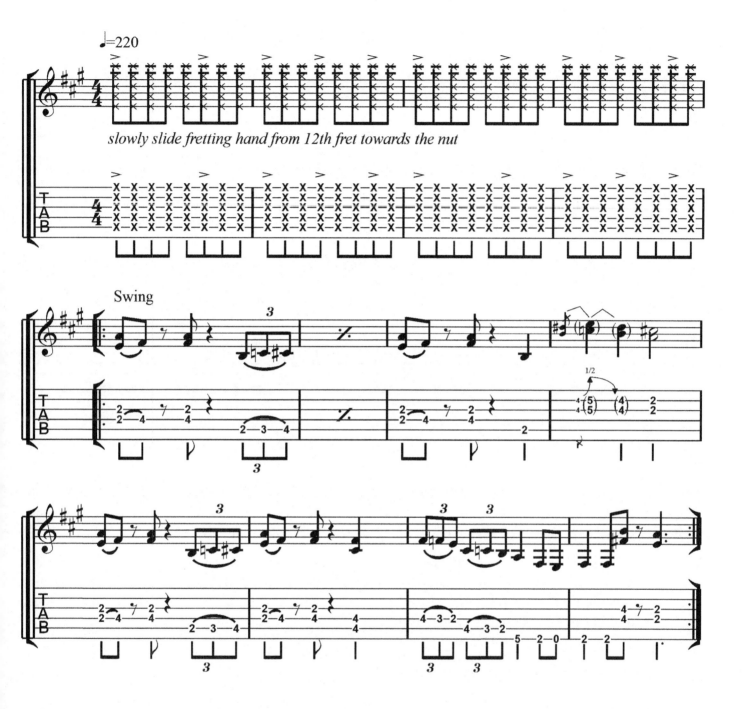

slowly slide fretting hand from 12th fret towards the nut

Swing

Finally, having said phasers work best on clean tones, it's important to experiment and discover the range of sounds available for yourself. Here's what happens when a phaser is applied to a thick, distorted riff. Set the depth quite shallow and the rate slower, otherwise "cracks" will begin to appear in the wall of sound if the phasing is too deep! The aim is to add just a dash of pearlescence to an already intricate part.

Maintain alternate picking throughout the example. It's quite technical, so break it down bar-by-bar at first. Use the 2nd finger to fret the high C in bar two, otherwise keep a one-finger-per-fret rule until bar four where a brief position shift is easiest to execute.

Example 3c

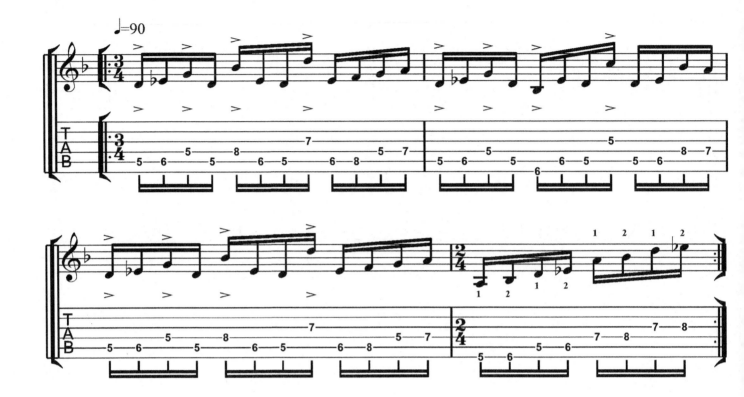

Flanger

A flanger is similar to a phaser, but has a far more pronounced sweeping effect and is often likened to a "whooshing" jet aeroplane sound effect. The reason it is much more dramatic is because the effect is caused by modulating the whole guitar signal, rather than just certain isolated frequency bands.

Like phasers, the flanger splits the guitar signal. Instead of phase inverting, one signal is slightly delayed by about 10ms. This is far too short to be audibly perceived as a delay, but the time separation causes similar phase cancellation to occur. The characteristic jet plane sweep is caused by the delay time of the wet signal being lengthened and then shortened. The rate and depth are again controlled by an LFO.

Regardless of the science, the only way to tell phasers and flangers apart is simply by listening to them side by side and observing the distinct character of each.

The name comes from the edges (flanges) of the tape spools on reel-to-reel tape machines, which was how the effect was first created. Engineers would record two tapes playing the same audio simultaneously and push or drag the spools to speed up or delay one tape in order to create the phase separation. Examples of studio tape flanging can be heard on The Small Faces' *Itchycoo Park* and the end of Hendrix's *Bold as Love*.

Flanger pedals can only partially recreate the original tape effect. As the effect is applied in real time, the modulated signal cannot be placed ahead of the dry signal without seeing into the future.

RATE is the speed of the sweeping sound, meaning how quickly the wet signal moves between the shortest and longest delay length.

DEPTH refers to the maximum delay time. A longer delay puts the two signals more out of phase and therefore cancels more of the affected frequencies.

LEVEL is less common that the first two controls, but balances the relative volume of the two signals. A 50:50 mix is fairly normal. Hearing only either signal makes the effect inaudible.

RESONANCE is a feedback loop that sends a variable amount of the wet signal back through the unit repeatedly to reprocessed, producing a more intense effect.

To start with, the sound of the flanger is presented over a typical '80s rhythm guitar riff. The guitar part would serve perfectly well within a song without the effect, but the flanger adds an extra level of interest, suitable to add variety to a second verse.

Set the flanger to a moderately slow rate and a low level. You don't want the swooshing texture to smother the articulate pick attacks, so start with the effect at zero and bring it up until it is present in the mix, but not overwhelming.

Example 3d

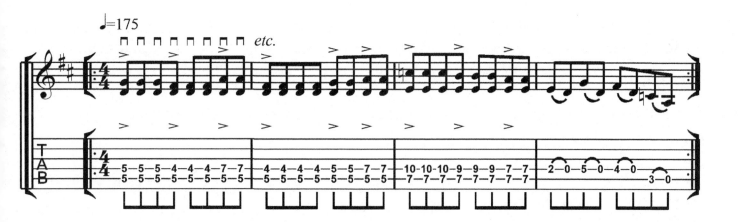

Most flangers do not feature a tap tempo control, but given the slow rates of sweep possible, it may be desirable to sync the filter's oscillation to the tempo of your music. For the second example, each bar just has one held chord and the flanger's rate control has been carefully adjusted so that the sweep switches direction on each bar.

Example 3e

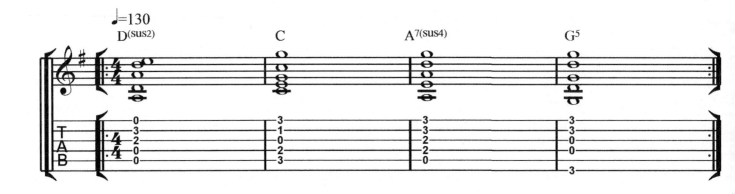

The third example demonstrates the flanger used on a heavy riff in Drop D tuning. Prominent flanging thins out the guitar's tone because frequencies are being lost to phase cancellation. Hence, it works well as an intro or bridge, before kicking into a full-band restatement.

Try using the pedal's mix knob (if it has one) or, alternatively, splitting the signal and directing only a portion of the sound to the flanger to make the effect more subtle, which will retail more of the body of the sound.

Example 3f

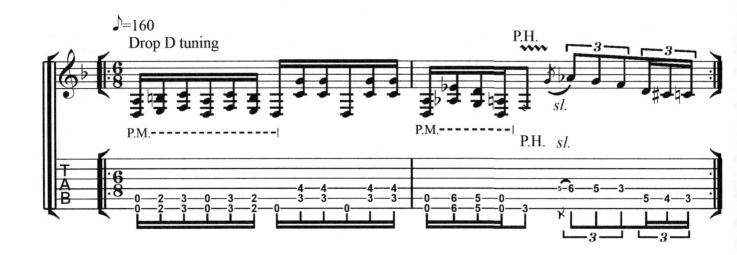

Chorus

Nothing evokes '80s pop-rock more than a clean chorused guitar part. Despite its past abuses, chorus can add depth and colour to your guitar tone, and will do so more subtly than the two modulations we've looked at so far.

When instruments or voices try to play in perfect unison there are always very slight tuning and timing differences – the result of which is to thicken the overall sound. Chorus tries to recreate this by delaying and retuning the signal, playing it back slightly faster or slower than the original.

The delays are longer than those used in a flanger, but still much shorter than can be perceived as separate sounds (about 30ms). The speed of playback alters the pitch. Slowing waves down lowers the pitch since the waves are being stretched, much like playing a 33rpm vinyl record back at 45rpm, or dragging on the turntable (don't try this at home kids!)

To avoid just sounding permanently out of tune, the chorus pedal then modulates the amount of delay and pitch deviation using an LFO, which keeps the degree of separation between the wet and dry paths constantly varied.

A natural chorus effect occurs with 12-string guitars and acoustic pianos, since each pair of strings will always be fractionally out of tune.

The first standalone chorus unit was **Roland's CE-1**, released in 1976. This large pedal extracted the chorus effect built into their already popular Jazz-Chorus 120 amplifier. The JC-120 has remained hugely popular to this day as a crystal-clear solid-state amp, particularly with metal bands who use it for clean tones.

Phase, flange and chorus effects have identically labelled controls, but for each effect type they manipulate a different parameter.

RATE on a chorus pedal controls how quickly the signal moves from in-tune to most detuned. This is the frequency of the LFO.

DEPTH sets the limit for how much the signal is detuned by, dictated by the amplitude of the LFO wave.

MIX is the balance of the signals. Mix in the delayed, detuned signal for a more intense chorus.

There's only one place to start with chorus and that's with the boys in blue. Here's a classic Andy Summers inspired idea. Let it ring by holding the chord shapes where possible. Also palm mute slightly, but keep the attack crisp. Andy Summers used the original **Roland CE-1** before migrating to the compact **BOSS CH-1**.

The second half of the example demonstrates how the chorus sounds with sustained chords. The extended 7th and 9th voicings betray Summers' jazz background. With the chorus swirling away, they have a strong fusion vibe.

Example 3g

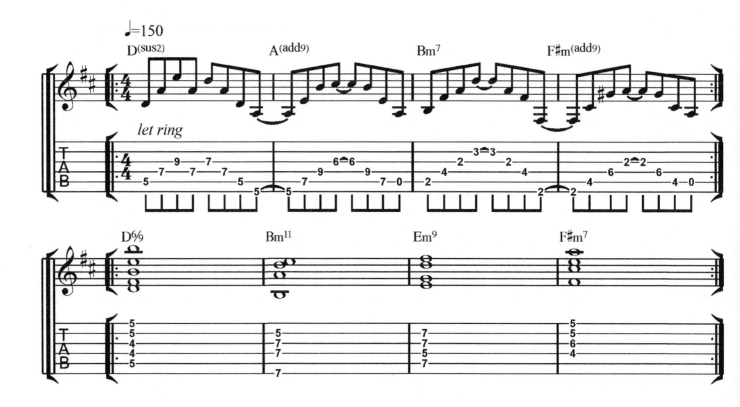

The Boss chorus pedals, much like the JC-120, offer great clarity and precision, but if you're chasing a grungier sound then other analogue choruses such as **Electro-Harmonix's Small Clone** will give a thicker tone. The single-coil pickup and Small Clone place our next riff firmly in '90s Seattle.

Example 3h

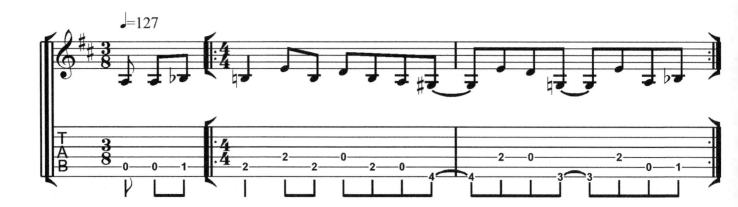

Some metal guitarists have applied chorus to their rhythm tones. Chorus helps to spread the sound and make it fatter, in the same way that doubling the performance would in the studio. It works best for big chunky riffs rather than fast intricate ones.

Mute the unused strings carefully while playing the natural harmonics or they'll lose the purity and contrast to the low notes.

Example 3i

'90s Nu-metal fused alternative rock and metal with hip-hop, whose electronic influence created interesting textures rather than intricate guitar parts. For this example, the depth and rate of the chorus effect have been turned up to maximum. This more pronounced detuning and rapid oscillation creates the otherworldly sound effect.

The result is definitely more unsettling than ethereal, so it's unsurprising that you find many strange modulation effects in tracks by the band KoRn to augment their music's moody, murky style.

Recorded on Earthquaker Devices' appropriately named **Sea Machine**, this example uses its additional controls of Shape, Dimension and Animate to leave Davy Jones himself feeling a bit pallid.

Example 3j

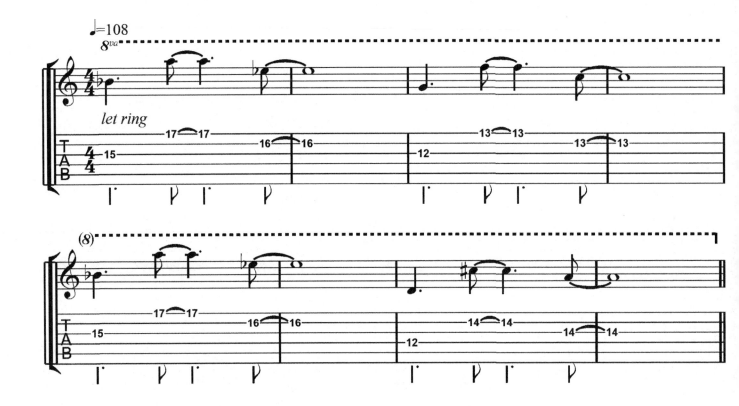

Tremolo

The first three types of modulation (phaser, flanger and chorus) all use roughly the same process of splitting the guitar signal and then messing with one of them, causing phase interference when mixed back together. Thankfully, tremolo is much simpler to understand and can be demonstrated by just turning your guitar's volume control up and down rapidly while holding a chord.

A tremolo pedal is just that! A volume control operated by an LFO. The speed and shape of the LFO wave controls the fade in/out of volume, from a gradual swell to straight flicks between fully on and fully off.

Big Bill Broonzy's playing on *You Can't Do That Do Me* by Roosevelt Sykes (1942) is one of the first examples of guitar effects, and features tremolo from about the middle of the song onwards. The earliest effect box was the fascinating **DeArmond** tremolo that used a shaking tank of fluid to cause the changes in volume.

I'd like to clear up a misconception at this point, brought about by Fender's mislabelling of their equipment. The "vibrato" on some amplifiers is in-fact tremolo, rather than vibrato. A vibrato causes changes in pitch (incidentally another type of effect pedal). Likewise, the "tremolo" arm on Stratocasters should be correctly termed a vibrato arm, since it affects pitch, not volume.

The controls on a tremolo pedal are most commonly:

RATE – you know the drill! Tremolo is more likely to be synced up to the tempo than other modulation effects, so rate will often be marked with specific note values and a tap-tempo.

DEPTH is very simply the minimum volume in the trough of each pulse. This could be a slight dip, or total silence.

SHAPE as with phasers, dictates the shape of the LFO wave. A rounded sine wave creates a gradual ebb and flow of volume, while a steep-sided square wave flicks between minimum and maximum levels.

The tremolo effect was often used in the James Bond soundtracks and has become a useful and widely recognised cliché in popular culture. The secret "00" chord progression and augmented chords in the following passage are completed by the touch of light tremolo.

The tremolo rate is quite slow, so each pulse lasts over a few notes. Avoid setting the tremolo too fast or deep when playing more intricate pieces, as this can cut out some notes almost completely. As with the flanger in Example 3e, use the level control to mix in the appropriate amount of wet signal.

The clean channel of the amp should be on the edge of breaking up, so turn the gain up until big strummed chords sound a little overdriven.

As well as film scores, you can hear the "spy tone" in the music of trip-hop band Portishead.

Example 3k

In contrast to the previous example, sometimes cutting out the sound completely is exactly what is wanted and the effect becomes the main element of the sound. Here the depth has been set to maximum, so the bottom of each trough is silence.

In the next example I used a boutique **DLS Effects Stereo Tremolo** which is based on the classic purple Dunlop Tremolo pedal. The "shape" control changes the LFO from a sine to a square wave. The shape is set to "square" meaning that the volume flicks almost instantly between zero and maximum.

This type of tremolo often forms the main groove of a song. Having the speed out-of-sync with the song will sound awful and make it very difficult to play against, so having a tremolo with a tap-tempo feature is essential. To get the 1/8th note pulse, the tremolo was set to pulse twice as fast as the given tempo.

A good illustration of this technique is R.E.M.'s *Crush with Eyeliner* where the tremolo guitar part sets up the whole song.

If you're using a multi-fx, the millisecond speeds are calculated using the same process as in the delay chapter.

Example 3l

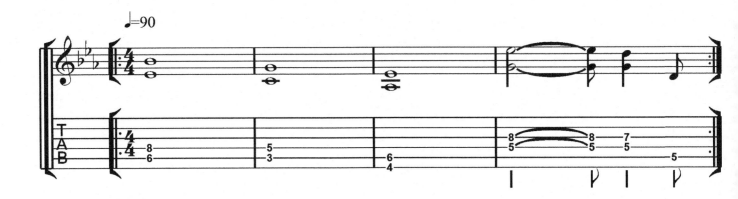

In other situations, being out of time can be appropriate. You can even manipulate the effect in real time to create an accelerating or decelerating pulse. The twin-guitar intro to *Bones* by Radiohead has two tremolos, each at their own speed, before the rates start to slow down.

Some pedals have an input for an expression pedal, otherwise you'll have to reach down and turn the pots by hand. Thankfully this technique works best with sustained sounds, so your picking hand should be temporarily unemployed. The following example can be played without the need for an expression pedal.

On the final chord, I also used the depth pot to make the oscillations shallower, so that the tremolo appears to "melt" back into the ringing chord as it slows down.

Example 3m

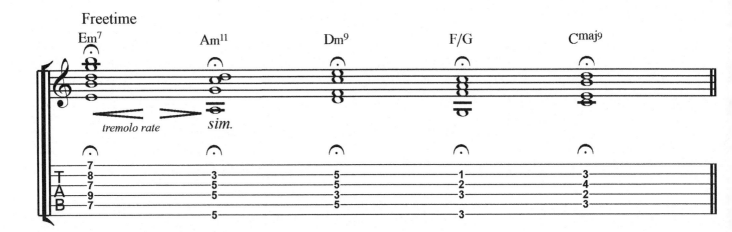

A slicer effect is essentially a very aggressive tremolo effect that gates the signal i.e. it allows through either all or no signal. The settings are similar to Example 3l but with a stream of fast notes played, rather than a sustained chord.

For this apocalyptic dissonant tapping lick, the slicer is set to pulse on 1/16th notes, or 4x the tempo. The result is that the natural envelope of each note is truncated, leaving the guitar sounding more like a synth or glitchy computer.

To achieve maximum impact, the timing of the 1/16th notes needs to be watertight, so practise the lick slowly to a metronome before speeding it up. To hear a "dying computer" slicer check out the guitar solo on Meshuggah's *Future Breed Machine*.

Example 3n

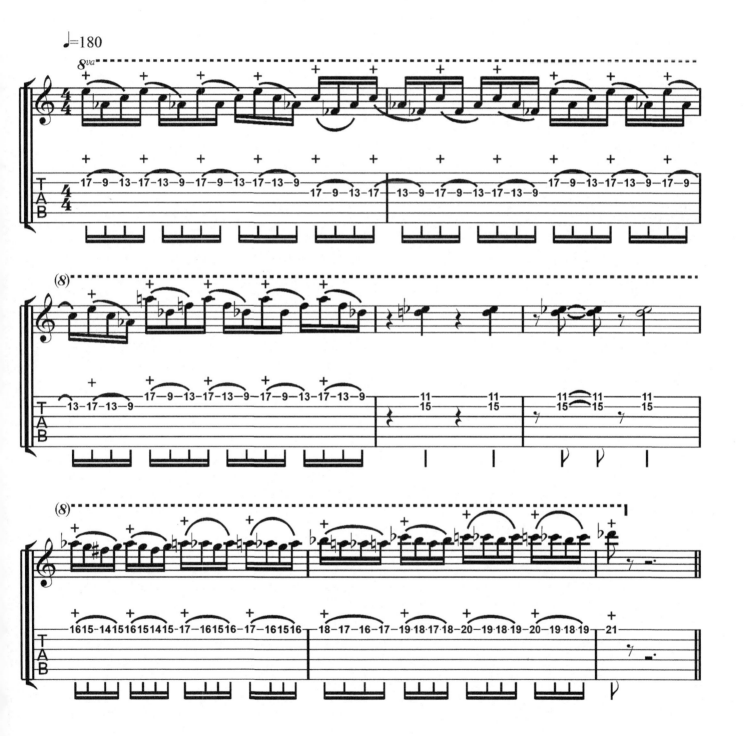

Recommended Listening:

Phaser:

Led Zeppelin – *In My Time of Dying*
Waylon Jennings – *Luchenbach, Texas*
Pink Floyd – *Shine on You Crazy Diamond*
Dream Theater – *In the Presence of Enemies Pt. 1*
Ozzy Osbourne – *Bark at the Moon* (solo)

Flanger:

Heart – *Barracuda*
Lenny Kravitz – *Are You Gonna Go My Way* (pre-solo riff)
Rush – *The Spirit of Radio*
Extreme – *It ('s a Monster)* (intro chords)
Black Label Society – *Crazy Horse*

Chorus:

The Police – *Message in a Bottle*
Nirvana – *Come as You Are*
Mike Stern – *Little Shoes*
Machine Head – *Imperium*
Vieux Farka Toure – *Fafa*

Tremolo:

The Shadows – *Apache*
Green Day – *Boulevard of Broken Dreams*
Audioslave – *Cochise*
Nancy Sinatra – *Bang Bang (My Baby Shot Me Down)*
The Smiths – *How Soon is Now?* (created by four Fender Twins' vibrato channels)

Chapter Four: The Crying Machine – Wah-wah & Envelope Filters

Ever since its invention in 1966, the wah-wah pedal has been one of the most expressive tools for electric guitarists. The vowel-like sounds it can produce brings the guitar closer to imitating the human voice.

The Vox Company stumbled on the effect when trying to cut costs on their amps for the American market, and the pedal format was the vision of session guitarist Del Casher.

Most guitar effects are set up beforehand then switched on or off as needed. The wah-wah is one of the few that you have to "play" in real time.

At its core, the wah is similar to a guitar's tone control, but it acts over a wider frequency range.

There are several types of filters used on sounds. The tone control on your guitar is a *low-pass* filter, meaning it removes all frequencies above a given threshold. As the tone knob is turned the threshold is lowered, removing more and more high and high-mid range frequencies.

In contrast, a wah-wah is a *band-pass* filter. Unlike high and low-pass filters, a band-pass has two thresholds and acts on frequencies that fall in the range between them, as shown in Figure 4a.

Fig. 4a Graph of the full frequency spectrum in a signal, and the range upon which the bandpass filter is acting

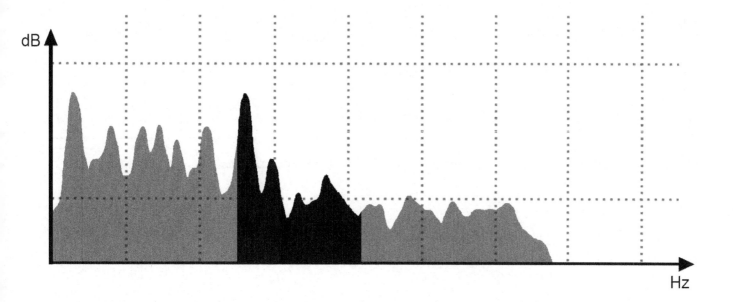

As the expression pedal on the wah is rocked back and forth, the band moves up and down through the frequency range and boosts the volume of that frequency band.

The upshot of this is an extremely vocal effect, with different positions on the frequency spectrum creating different vowel sounds, just like when you change the shape of your mouth. In essence, your vocal chords are a tone-generator and your mouth is an envelope filter!

To hear just how human the guitar can sound with a wah, listen to Steve Vai's "utterances" at the start of *The Audience is Listening*, and David Lee Roth's *Yankee Rose*, where Diamond Dave and Vai's guitars have a brief chat.

All the examples in this section were recorded with a **Dunlop Crybaby**, popular with Slash, Dimebag Darrell, Zakk Wylde and countless others. Hendrix used the original **Vox Wah**, while Steve Vai has a signature version of the **Morley Power Wah**, called **Bad Horsie**.

Being able to move the wah pedal perfectly in time with your strumming is one of the often overlooked skills of pop, rock and funk styles. To start with, here are two 1/16th note groove exercises, just using muted "scratch chords" by laying the fretting hand across the strings to stop them ringing.

The first has the accents on each beat, played by rocking the wah pedal forward to boost the high frequencies. This should feel just like tapping your foot in time with the music, but it may highlight inaccuracies in your playing if you've not consciously practised it before.

The pedal position is notated above each musical example. An "**o**" indicates fully forward or "open" position, and a cross "**+**" indicates the fully back or "closed" position.

Example 4a

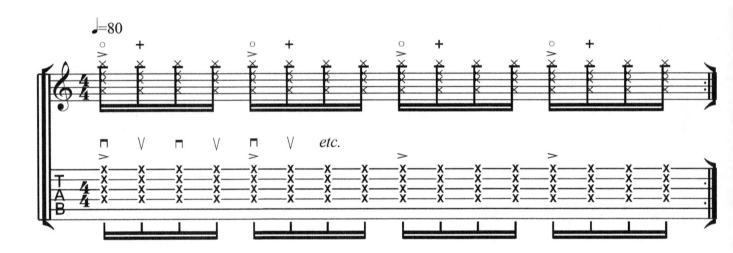

The second pattern places the accents on offbeat 1/8th notes, which to begin with is less intuitive. Count carefully to ensure accuracy and evenness. Recording yourself and listening back is a great practice method to highlight where you need to improve.

Example 4b

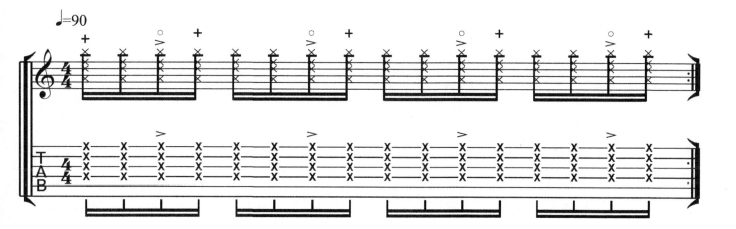

With the basics covered, the next musical example demonstrates the classic wacka-wacka effect that countless guitarists have used – perhaps most famously on Hendrix's intro to *Voodoo Child*. The rhythms can be improvised and should be syncopated to make things interesting, but focus on maintaining the underlying 1/16th feel throughout.

The trickiest rhythms will be when up-strums are accenting, corresponding to the off-beat 1/16th notes of each beat (1 **e** & **a**)

Example 4c

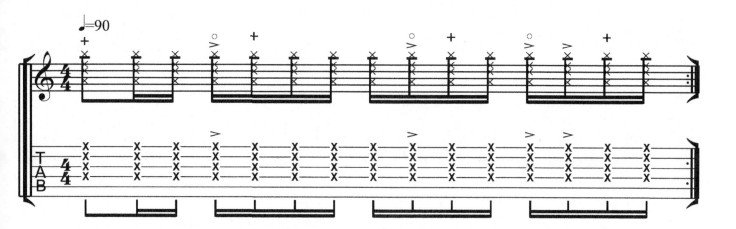

Next, actual chords are introduced. The muted strumming is still present, but the accents are now played with chords on the top strings. Keep the strings muted and just apply pressure to fret the chords momentarily, while at the same time rocking the wah forward.

The wah's high frequency boost adds an additional sense of light and shade to the chords and muted hits.

Example 4d

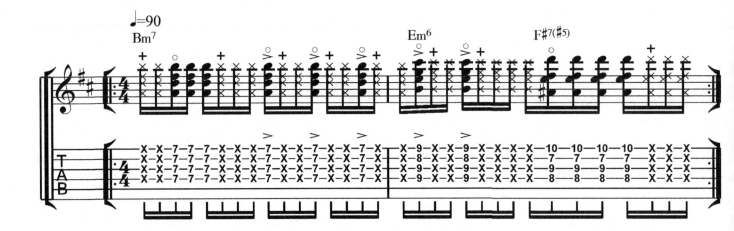

Now wah is used to give a gradual sweep to held chords. Much like modulation effects, the wah stops a static chord from feeling flat and lifeless, instead giving it direction.

Experiment with sweeping the pedal faster and slower. The longer the duration of the sweep, the more control you will need with your foot to make sure you don't run out of travel too soon.

Example 4e

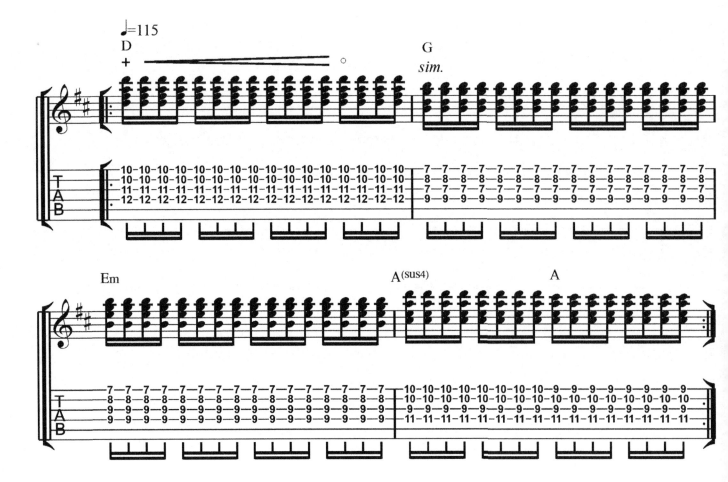

The last of our rhythm guitar examples is a driving rock riff. Wah pedals are not often used for low riffs, but here it adds extra rhythmic emphasis and makes the riff more striking and memorable. For a classic metal example listen to *Electric Funeral* by Black Sabbath, or Cliff Burton's snarling bass riff in *For Whom the Bell Tolls*.

Keep the first two power chords in each bar as short and detached as possible for maximum impact. Fret them with the first finger and lay the second and third down flat to mute in between.

Example 4f

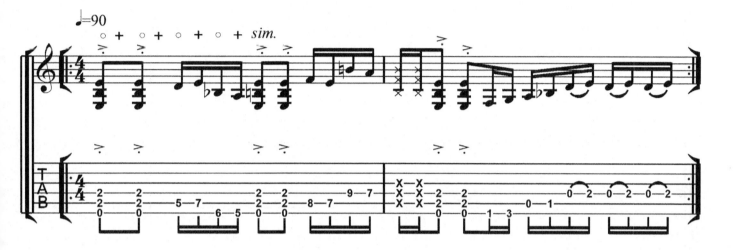

Now let's look at some lead guitar ideas. All of these licks are played with a distorted tone from the amp, with the wah placed at the front of the signal chain and followed by a **Tubescreamer**.

The first phrase is typical of the expressive lead playing of Slash, Dimebag Darrell and Zakk Wylde who all use the wah pedal to enhance their melodic playing, giving it a vocal-like quality. The wah should be opened on the most prominent notes in the phrases. These are usually the longer notes, ends of phrases, or ones that fall on strong beats.

Singing the melody and improvising the syllables will often give a good clue for where to open the wah.

A common mistake is to let the wah rock back and forth with the rhythm when soloing, because many players are used to tapping their foot to the beat and don't have the coordination or independence to break out of it. To start with, play melodically in free time to get the foot used to being in sync with your phrases rather than the underlying 1/4 note pulse.

Example 4g

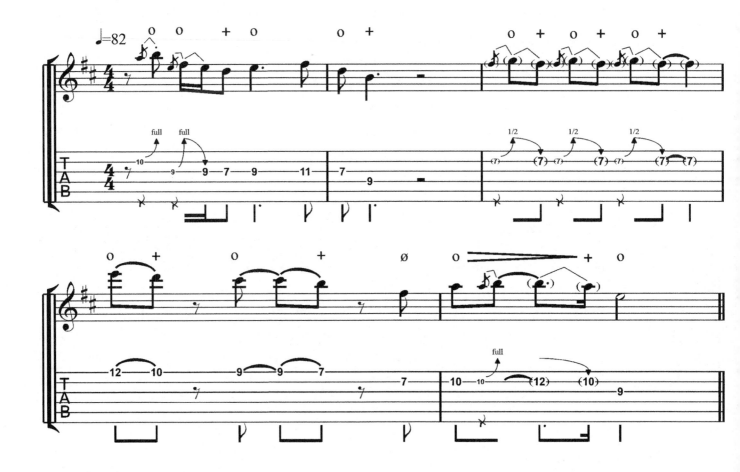

Lean forward on the pedal as you pick each bend to make it roar. Be sure to cut the note off before rocking the pedal back to the starting position before the next bend. Each string-bend should end with the wah still fully open.

The odd rhythmic phrasing and use of the diminished scale was inspired by prog-metallers Mastodon, who often employ bastardised country-guitar bends into their intricately composed songs.

Example 4h

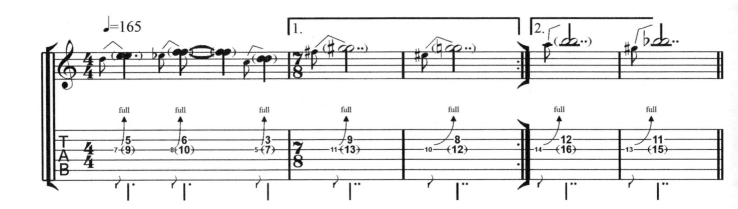

Rather than pick out specific "syllables" within a melodic phrase, the following example features fast, repeating licks in D minor. The wah is opened slowly over the course of each whole bar, then repeated in the following bar as the fast lick is moved to different notes in the scale. The effect means that there is a change of tone across the repeating pattern. The gradual opening out of the brightness adds a sense of approaching a climax.

The additional high frequencies from the pick attack will respond well to the wah, as do pinch harmonics so be sure to dig in hard with the one at the end of the phrase and use the wah to accent it as with Example 4g.

Example 4i

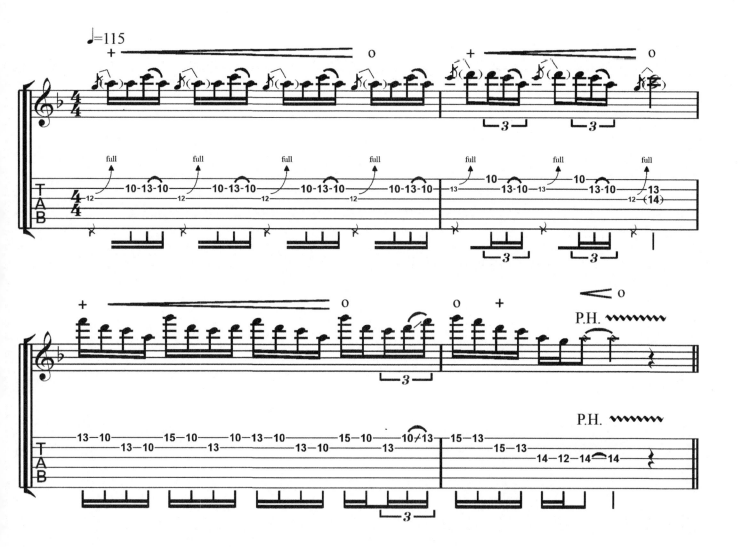

So far, I've demonstrated the wah as an expressive effect being actively operated in time with the music, but the next two examples leave it in a fixed position to create a very specific filtered tone.

The first is a reggae example and the guitar is played through a clean amp. The pedal is left fully open to filter the treble frequencies. The ever-present reggae "skank" guitar rhythm should be tightly percussive to cut through the mix and cement the groove. The wah's treble boost gives even more high-end presence. Select the bridge pickup and strum quite forcefully.

Example 4j

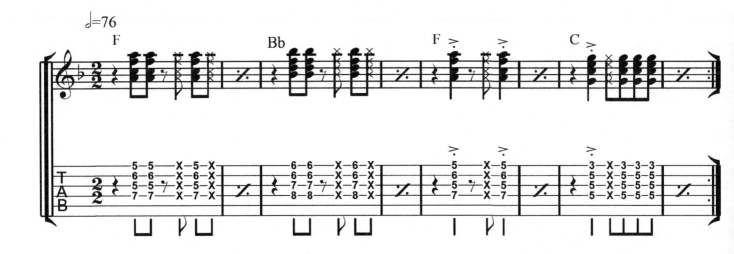

You should experiment with the sounds that the wah produces when left in different places along its travel. Another popular setting is half-open which gives a nasal quality by filtering out the bottom and top frequencies. This gives a very distinctive tone that Joe Satriani used to great effect on his classic track *Surfing with the Alien.*

This example features the synth-like nasal tone in the context of an E Lydian melody, featuring some slippery legato and sliding phrases.

Example 4k

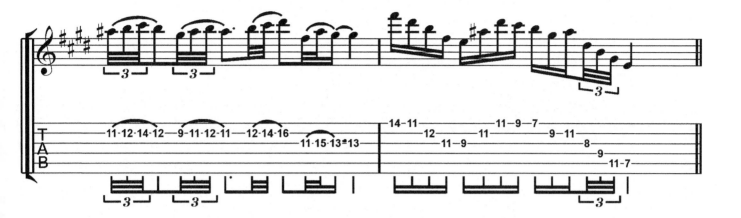

To close this chapter, here are two examples featuring an auto-wah, or envelope filter. As the name suggests, auto-wahs remove the expression pedal and the filter sweep is usually controlled by picking dynamics. The first models used circuitry plundered from synthesisers and put into a pedal.

This example was recorded with the envelope filter from a **Line6 POD HD500** and uses the guitarist's picking dynamics to control the wah's position. Picking harder will open the wah, whereas palm muting or lighter pick-strokes will close the wah. This will test your consistency to avoid accents popping out all over the place, but with practice you can achieve a very fluid and intuitive effect.

The constant alternate picked 1/16th note rhythm first of all accents the first note of each beat, then gradually crescendos, causing the wah to open out. Pick quite firmly throughout, but lower the pick into the strings more and more starting with a very shallow light touch to achieve the crescendo.

Example 41

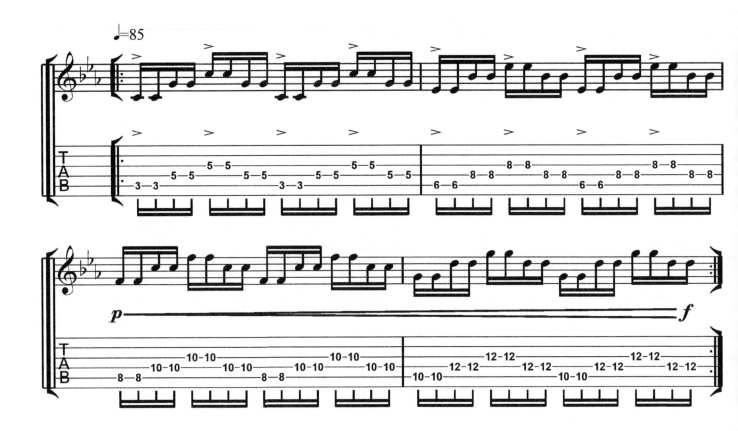

'70s funk bass guitar parts often featured autowah to give that distinctive "bubbling" sound, usually courtesy of the **Mu-Tron III**. The following riff imitates that feel on guitar. The effect is going to be consistent, so you can focus on getting the syncopated guitar part to really groove without having to worry about operating an expression pedal.

I used the slap bass technique to emulate the classic funk sound. For a great example of the slap technique on guitar, listen to Regi Wooten. The cross symbols here represent percussive hits with the fretting hand fingers. If you've not studied slapping, then a percussive alternate picking approach will also work well.

Listen to most Booty Collins track to hear the funky envelope filter bass tone, which greatly influenced Flea from Red Hot Chili Peppers.

Example 4m

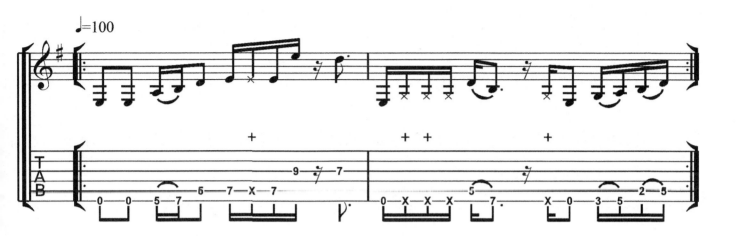

Recommended Listening for wah-wah use:

Jimi Hendrix – *Voodoo Child* (scratch intro)
Isaac Hayes – *Theme from "Shaft"* (gtr – Charles "Skip" Pitts)
Eagles – *Hotel California* (verse scratch part)

Bob Marley & the Wailers – *Stir It Up* (gtr 1: fixed open, gtr 2: slow sweep)
Metallica – *Enter Sandman* (solo)
Jeff Beck – *I Ain't Superstitious*
David Lee Roth/Steve Vai – *Yankee Rose* (intro "talking")

Dream Theater – *Home* (main riff)
Rage Against the Machine – *Bulls on Parade* (2nd riff)

Led Zeppelin – *Whole Lotta Love* (solo breaks, wah left fully open)
Frank Zappa - *I'm the Slime* (main melody, half open)
Joe Satriani – *Surfing with the Alien* (main melody, half open)

Pink Floyd – *Echoes* (seagull sounds at 13:45 by connecting the wah in reverse!)
Bootsy's Rubber Band – *I'd Rather Be with You* (Mu-Tron envelope filter)
The Prodigy – *Breathe* (envelope filter applied to guitar sample)

Chapter Five: Smack My Pitch Up – Pitch-shifters & Harmonisers

The effects in this chapter produce much more dramatic results than those examined so far. Extreme changes of pitch can take you out of the guitar's natural range, or make you not sound like a guitarist at all!

The chapter is divided into three sections:

-   Pitch shifts that move the pitch by a fixed interval.

-   So-called "intelligent harmonisers" that track your notes and change the interval to stay within a scale.

-   Expression-pedal pitch manipulation.

Pitch-Shifters

The earliest pitch effects were octave pedals. Because they're merely doubling or halving every frequency, they don't need to analyse the pitch content and often use analogue circuitry. The **Octavia** was originally made for Hendrix by his technician Roger Mayer. It adds a tone an octave above and can be first heard on the lead breaks in *Fire* and *Purple Haze*.

Rather than hearing a distinct second note, the Octavia provides searing high-frequency presence and bite to the lead tone that makes it cut right through a mix.

Example 5a

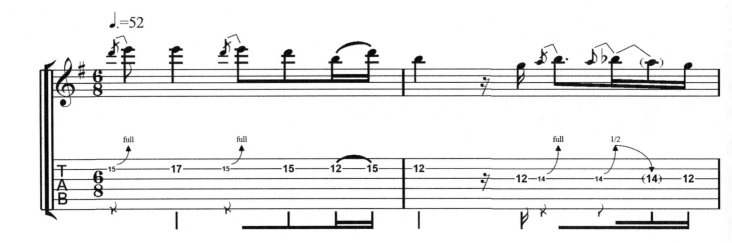

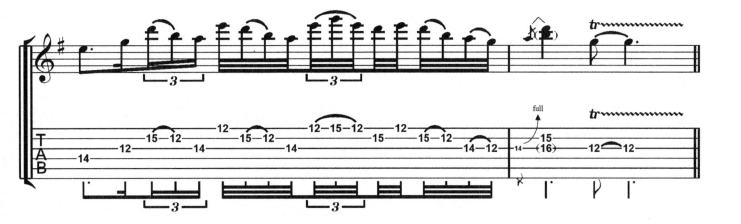

The second idea is inspired by garage rock's grindy fuzz-laden sound. An octave-down effect doubles the single-note riff an octave below – to play this passage in octaves with bends and vibrato would be too awkward.

The lower octave adds body when playing in the midrange of the guitar. A wide array of options opens up if you split the signal and use other effects to colour the direct guitar and octave note independently.

Jack White of The White Stripes sometimes uses an **Electro Harmonix POG** to thicken his sound in this way, allowing his guitar to fill the range usually allotted to guitar and bass.

I used the **Maui Maea** pedal by **KMA Machines** for this example. The pedal features an effects loop that affects the clean signal, to which I added a **Fuzz Face** to make the sound even fatter.

Example 5b

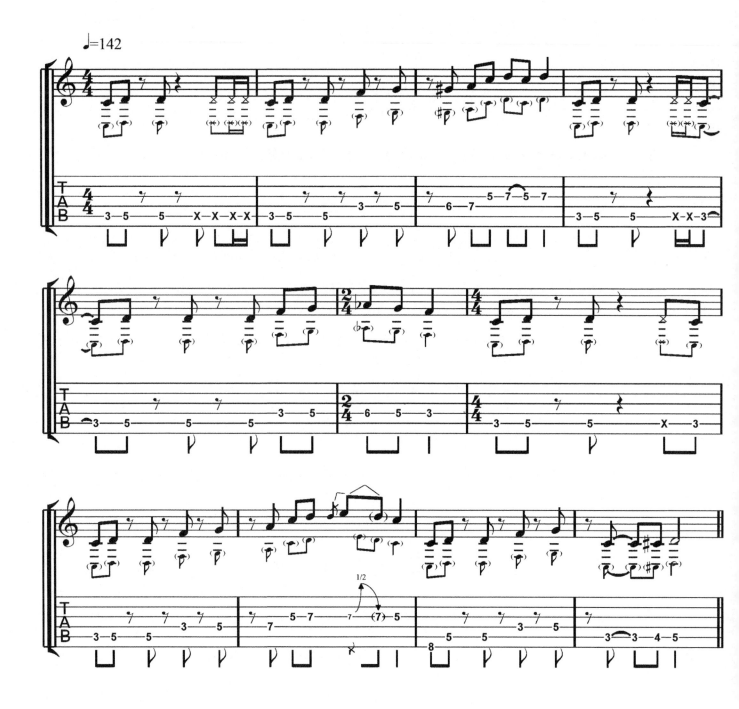

The third octave idea mixes out the direct signal so that the transposed down tone is more dominant. This is perfect if you need to cover a synth-bass role on guitar!

The **Maui Maea** has independent volume controls for each of the two octaves and one for the clean sound. The clean signal is turned down to 0, and the -1 and -2 octaves were balanced to taste.

Example 5c

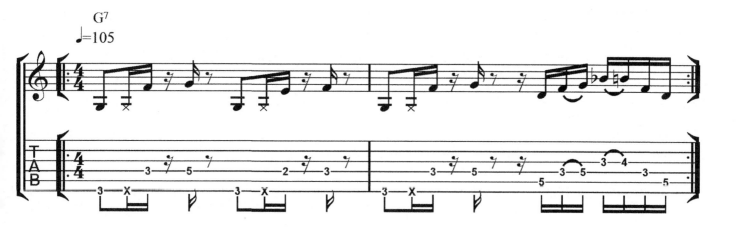

Analogue octave pedals, as used for examples 5a to 5c, are monophonic. Very precise technique is needed to stop the pedal glitching and getting confused.

Thankfully, more recent developments in digital effects have produced pitch-shifters that can track chords and faster playing, so we can choose whether to include the glitches for creative effect.

With a polyphonic octave pedal it's possible to imitate the paired strings of a 12-string guitar or mandolin.

The following example mixes the clean guitar with itself an octave higher. The high notes are mixed quietly enough so that their synthetic tone isn't distracting, but they still add a layer of high frequency sparkle to the chords.

To improve the impersonation, a detune effect or very short delay (50ms) could be added to replicate the chorusing effect of paired strings.

Example 5d

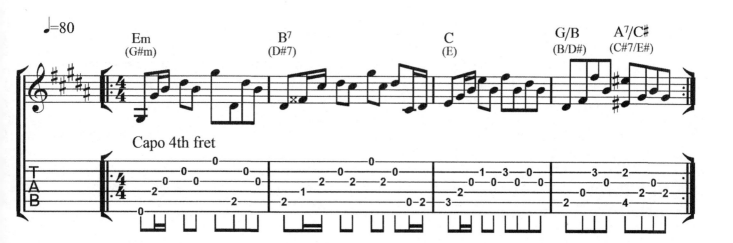

Intelligent Harmoniser

An intelligent harmoniser allows a solo guitarist to recreate several layers of guitar harmonies. They are also beneficial when harmonising with another guitarist in a two-guitar band. To play harmonies, it would mean that the rhythm guitar would have to be omitted, which would leave the texture sounding empty and weak.

One of the hardest parts of playing guitar harmonies is syncing up the speed of vibrato and bends with the other guitarist. Thankfully, the harmoniser will always get them right, giving you the freedom to improvise and embellish on the fly!

Discussing diatonic harmony in full is rather beyond the scope of this section, but here's a brief refresher to help explain what the harmoniser pedal is doing:

Every major scale contains seven pitches. The distance between the root note and each of the others is known as a 2nd, 3rd, 4th, right up to the 7th. Playing a supporting melody to the original one is known as *harmony* and these harmony parts will often be played a fixed distance from the original.

Here's an ascending C Major scale played in 3rds. This means the harmony starts on the 3rd step (E) and remains a third up from the main voice throughout.

Fig. 6a – Harmonised C Major scale with tab

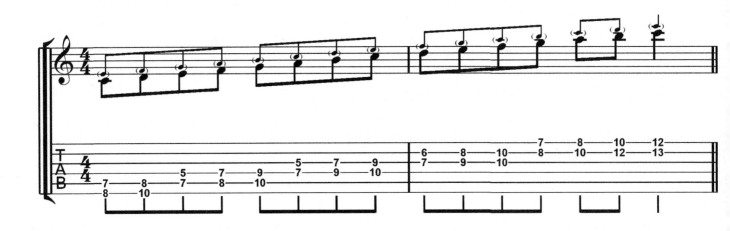

Each interval has its own sound and character. The most commonly used intervals for harmonisation are the sweet and pleasing 3rd and 6th intervals. The guitar harmony parts found in many bands like Thin Lizzy, Iron Maiden, Wishbone Ash and Mastodon are usually composed by stacking 3rds in this way.

The pattern of tones and semitones in the scale means the harmony changes between a major 3rd and minor 3rd depending on which note is played.

Having been programmed with the chosen key and desired interval, the harmoniser will analyse the pitch you play and produce the appropriate harmony to fit with the key.

Some harmonisers list both major and minor keys, but it's worth knowing how to work out the relative key to each one. Every major key shares the same set of seven notes with one minor key, which is found three semitones, or two steps down the scale.

E.g. G Major is relative to E Minor; F Major is relative to D Minor; and C Major is relative to A Minor.

If you'd like more information about the structure of keys, scales and intervals then check out **The Practical Guide to Modern Music Theory for Guitarists** also by Fundamental Changes.

I also discuss writing effective twin-guitar harmonies in my book **Progressive Metal Guitar**.

For this section, the tab contains the played notes, but the notation also shows the notes produced by the harmoniser with small note heads.

Our first example is in the key of E Minor. It's a typical melodic rock guitar theme doubled up a third by the harmoniser.

Example 5e

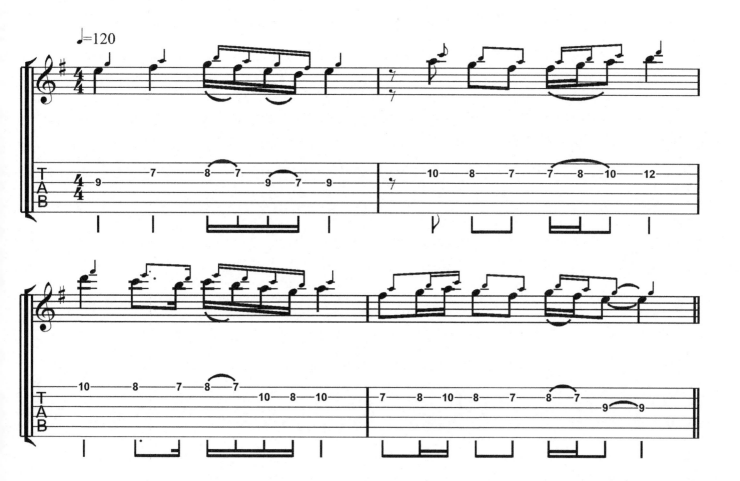

Playing up a 3rd from any given note or down a 6th both produce the same note, just an octave apart. For example, the note E is a 3rd above C (C D E), but it is also a 6th below C (C B A G F E).

The second example is similar to the first, but the harmoniser is set to play down a 6th. This means the interval is wider between the notes, and the original melody is on top, keeping it most prominent.

The same two notes are being heard, but the harmony is down an octave from the previous example.

Example 5f (NB: no tab for this example. It is played as Example 5e. Listen to the audio to hear how it should sound).

The next example is in the key of F Major and there are two harmonies added. This level of complexity is usually reserved for multi-fx or rack units, but could be achieved using two compact harmoniser pedals in parallel and splitting the signal with an A/B/Y box.

The first harmony is a diatonic 3rd above the melody, and the second is a 5th above the original note to create triads.

I have written the names of the chords formed over the stave.

Example 5g

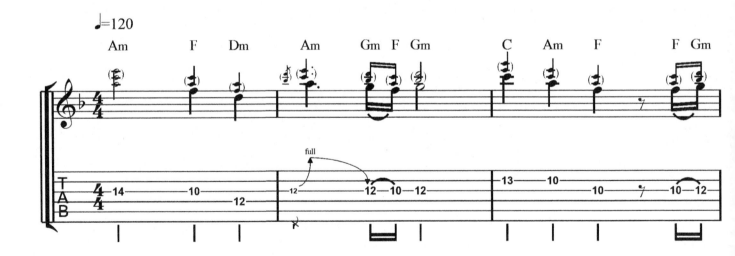

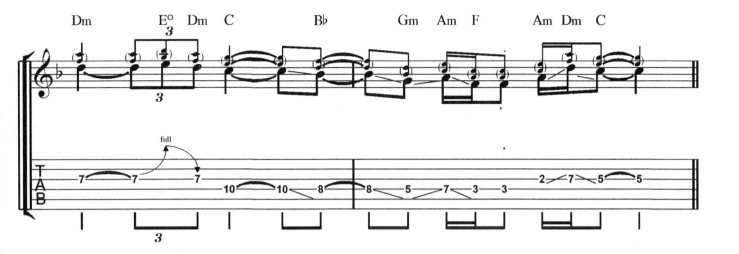

Notes in a chord can be reordered to create inversions (chords where the root isn't at the bottom), which sometimes produces a more pleasing sound. In the previous example, the 3rd-above harmony added more colour, while the 5th-above just added thickness. This time the fifth has been reshuffled to the bottom. A 5th above is the same as playing the note a 4th below, so now the harmoniser is programmed to +3 and -4.

Example 5h (NB: no tab for this example. It is played as Example 5g. Listen to the audio to hear how it should sound).

It would be rude not to include the third common variation, which is to put both harmonies below the original, which would be -4 and -6. In the context of a band, this version would be more subtle. The melody would still be the dominant tune and the harmonies would be supportive, thickening the texture from below.

Try the three options over the same melodies to hear the difference.

Example 5i (NB: no tab for this example. It is played as Example 5g. Listen to the audio to hear how it should sound).

No matter which inversion you use, it's always safest to treat the melody as the root note of each harmony, even it is the top or middle note. This way you're less likely to create harmonies that clash with the rest of the music.

Finally, here's a useful variation that combines the sweetness of a 3rd harmony with the thicker texture of an octave-below. While the previous three examples give the initial melody enough strength to stand alone, it may be overbearing in a bigger band situation. This approach reduces the harmonic information while still allowing the melody to sound huge and impressive.

Example 5j (NB: no tab for this example. It is played as Example 5g. Listen to the audio to hear how it should sound).

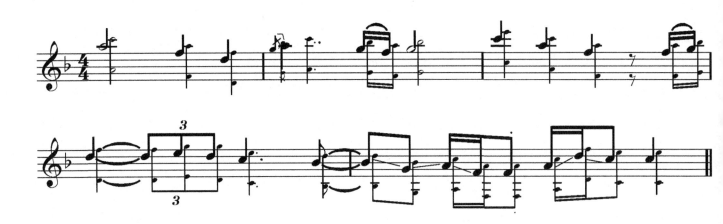

Expression Pedal Pitch-shift

The iconic **Digitech Whammy** pedal, first released in 1989, made real-time pitch shifting possible. Many players have used it to create wild and otherwise impossible sounds.

The original versions were not polyphonic, so would introduce glitches when receiving more than one note. Radiohead's Johnny Greenwood embraced this short-coming on their track *My Iron Lung.* The noisy artefacts arising from letting notes ring together gives a darker maniacal tone to chiming arpeggios that would otherwise sound innocuously pretty.

Set the pitch shifter up an octave and, if there is the option, set it to monophonic or "classic" mode rather than polyphonic or "chords".

Example 5k

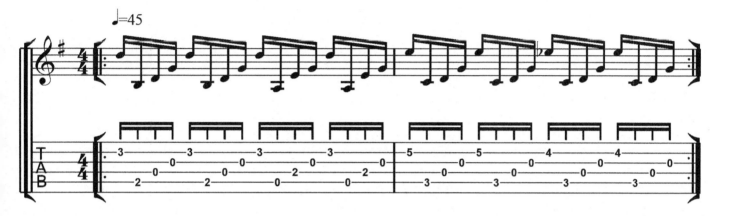

From Johnny Greenwood to Dimebag Darrell…

The next whammy riff rockets between skull-crushingly heavy power chords and screaming fills. The whammy pedal is set to two octaves up and the effect is somewhere between a pinch harmonic and a synthesizer. Heavily palm muted power chords and a wide vibrato on the accented notes will heighten the contrast.

Be sure to work on this one slowly at first. Like the wah examples, it will take some practice to get rhythmic control of the expression pedal. Aim to hear as little of the actual slide as possible by moving it in the rests. Alternatively, you could set the pedal in the forward position and repeatedly press the on/off button to activate the pitch-shift.

Example 5l

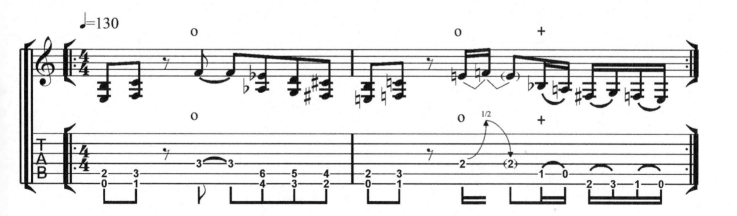

Tom Morello is perhaps the guitarist most closely associated with the Whammy. His radical approach to lead guitar was well suited to the hip hop/metal style of Rage Against the Machine and mid-90s nu-metal. Morello uses unconventional techniques to imitate car-alarms, helicopters and a range of textural sound effects. As Tom himself says, he was "designated the band's DJ" and was inspired by the synths and samples in gangster rap, rather than typical guitar-heroes.

Here are four typical sound effect ideas that show just how outlandish the Whammy pedal can be.

In Example 5m, the pedal is set at +8ve throughout, and is set to *classic* or monophonic.

The first part also uses a kill-switch on the guitar. This cuts the sound and is used to produce stuttering rhythmic patterns. Strum all the open strings and play the rhythm on the switch as notated. The Whammy glitches and distorts because of the polyphonic input to produce the white-noise sound.

If your guitar doesn't have a kill-switch (and unless you're a fan of RATM or Buckethead why would it?!) then Les Paul style controls with separate volume controls for each pickup and a selector switch will do the job. Failing that, strumming the rhythm and muting very carefully with the fretting hand in between will get fairly close.

The second half plays something slightly more recognisable as a guitar solo. Depress the pedal for each harmonic as you pick it, so that it shoots up an octave, then rock the pedal back and forth in 1/8th notes as indicated while tremolo picking each note. The tab shows what you're actually playing and the notation depicts the audible result.

The last phrase goes back to the kill-switch to be authentic to Tom's approach (but normal alternate picking is fine). The notation is approximate, just begin to slow down independently to the track and simultaneously release the pedal slowly. The result is a slow-motion tape/vinyl effect.

Example 5m

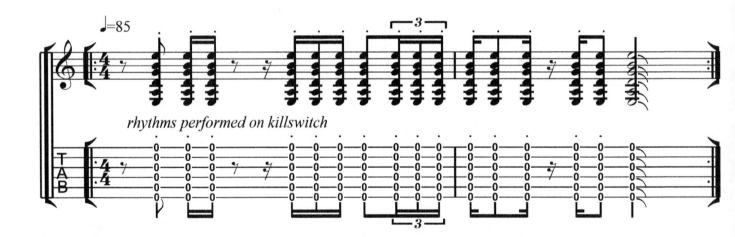

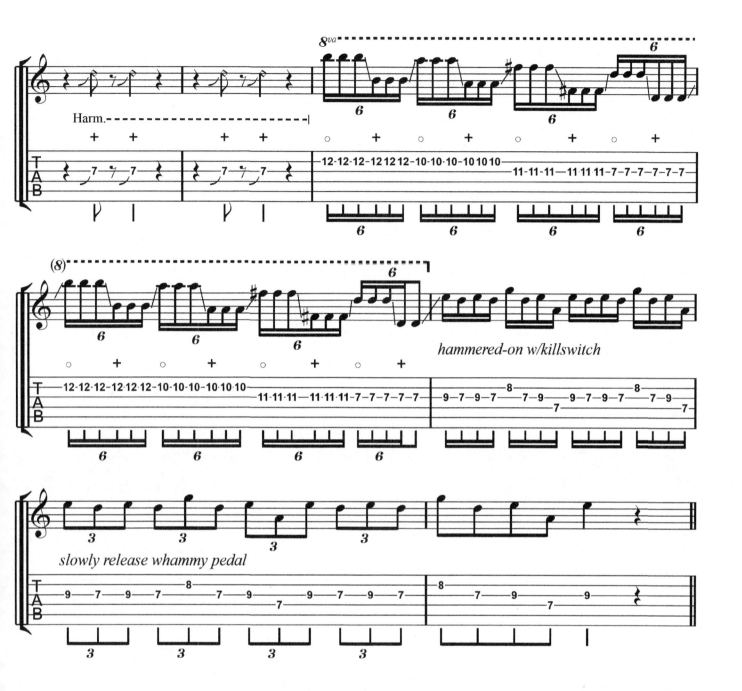

Another great exponent of whammery is Jack White, especially in his work with The White Stripes. Despite the duo's retro image, they weren't afraid of using modern gear to augment their raw garage-blues sound.

Jack sets the Whammy to transpose down an octave to play bass register parts such as in the famous *Seven Nation Army* riff. For his characteristic lead tone, the pedal is set to two-octaves up. This piercing synth-like tone introduces big sweeping slides to his licks on tracks such as *Ball and Biscuit*, adding to the manic and noisy soundscape.

The following example uses a question-and-answer idea between chord stabs and lead breaks. This technique is effective at filling in space in the duo format, where continuous single note solos would sound empty and exposed.

Set the effect to play up two octaves when the pedal is fully forward and zero when the pedal is back. Rock it forward for the fills as notated. The third and fourth fills make more expressive use of the Whammy.

The guitar part itself is very traditional to old blues, using open chords and an open position E minor pentatonic box shape, but the fuzz and pitch shifter give them a new slant.

Example 5m

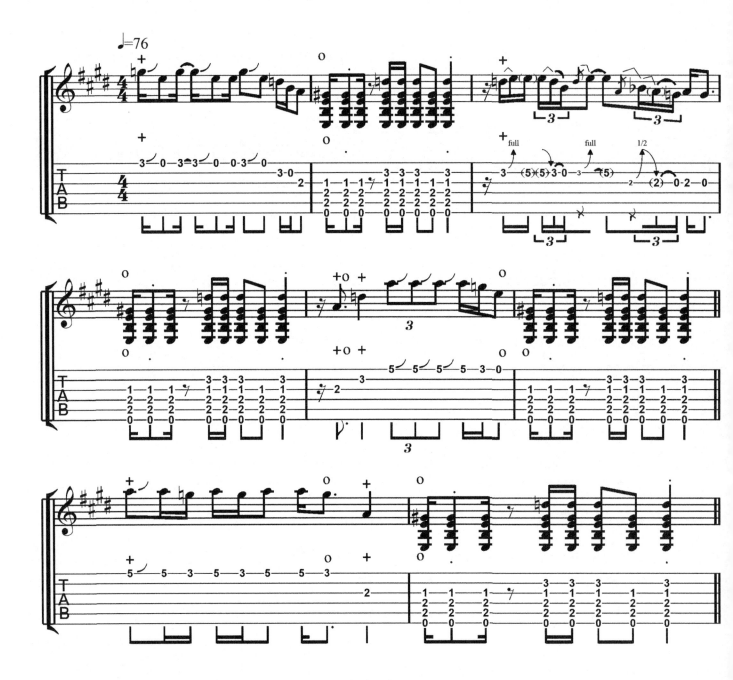

David Gilmour is also a fan of the Whammy pedal. As a purveyor of understated and tasteful guitar playing, it's perhaps surprising that Gilmour should favour a pedal generally associated with lairy pyrotechnics. But his subtle use of the pedal extends his already impressive string bending range. The pedal's first appearance is on *The Division Bell* (1994) and he has continued to use it, albeit sparingly, on subsequent projects.

Gilmour's playing is always pristinely articulated, so avoid the pedal adding any unwanted glitches by bending carefully and muting the other strings. The pedal is used to transition between normal and stratospherically high phrases, or to glissando dramatically out of held notes.

Over the course of the example, the whammy pedal is gradually introduced. I start with a single glide up on the end of a note, before playing whole phrases in the 8ve-up position, then finishing with a sequenced pattern using big sweeps up and down.

Example 5n

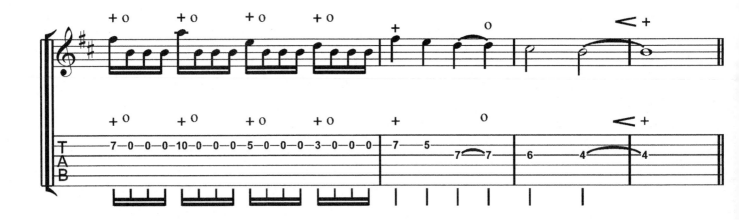

The next example isn't based on any individual's style, but demonstrates how you might imitate a pedal steel without the use of a slide. Beautiful clean chords being slid and bent is central to the pedal steel style, so the whammy pedal must be set in polyphonic mode. The pitch-shift is set to +4th this time.

The fourth transposition allows chords to remain within the key, for example C slides up to F, and G slides up to C. The borrowed D major chord in bar five is shifted to G major quickly enough for it not to offend.

To make the glissandos sound as musical as possible takes more control than the rapid rhythmic shifts of the previous examples. Concentrate on getting a smooth gradual slide in bars one and eleven. The "half-open" symbol in bar eight is like a dip with a whammy bar – ease the pedal back just a little from the forward position.

Example 50

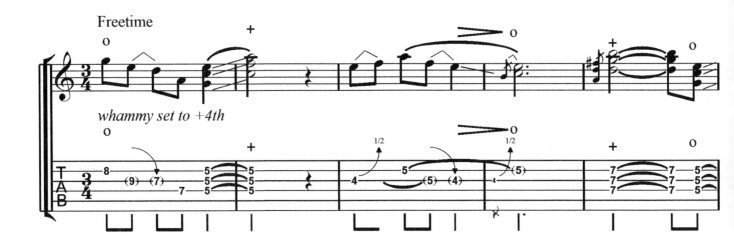

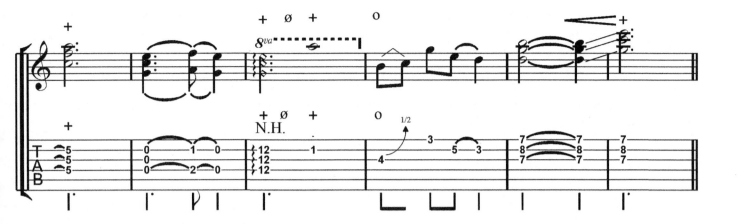

Back to the radical "in-yer-face" applications! Here, a short melodic fragment in A Harmonic Minor is shifted up, then down an octave and moved around the scale. Make the pedal movement as rapid as possible just before the downstroke of each new fragment. The slide will be audible, but not overly distracting.

Neoclassical players like Yngwie Malmsteen and Michael Romeo would play this lick by making lightning fast position shifts along the neck, but the Whammy version adds an interesting portamento effect between octaves, as well as being much easier to execute!

Example 5p

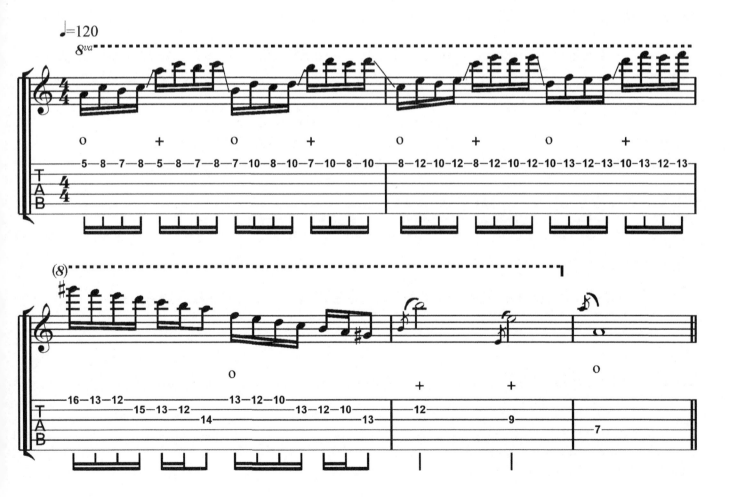

Finally, a similar idea to the previous one, but applied less strictly to a sweep-picked arpeggio. British power-metal band Dragonforce – never ones to take themselves too seriously – often use videogame inspired sounds in their songs, created on the guitars using slides, whammy bars, or effects.

Depress the pedal (set up an octave) as you reach the top of the sweep arpeggio and tremolo pick, and rock back and forth while performing the tapped arpeggio phrase, before sweeping back down and finally releasing the pedal to return to the original root note.

The wider overall range makes the arpeggio's contour even more dramatic, and the resulting jumble of notes at the top adds to Dragonforce's frenetic high-energy appeal.

To avoid confusion with the use of fret hand tapping, the whammy pedal positions are marked with ^ and v in this example.

Example 5q

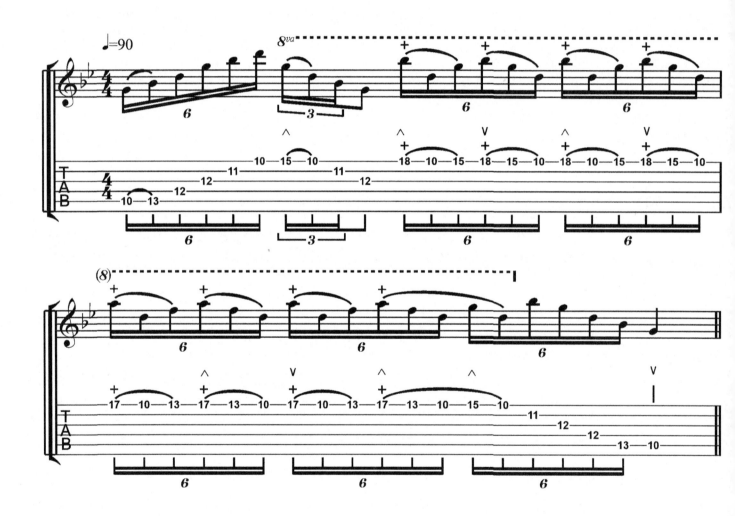

Placing harmonisers and pitch shifters early in the chain is the norm as it helps them analyse the input pitches, or "track" your playing, more accurately.

Placing them later will mean you can hear any time-based effects like reverb, delay or loop pedals get manipulated too. This is less conventional, but being able to slowly detune a series of delay repeats might be just the sound you're looking for!

Recommended Listening:

Jimi Hendrix – *Purple Haze* (solo)
Stevie Ray Vaughan – *Commit a Crime* (solo)
The White Stripes – *Blue Orchid*
Paul Gilbert – *(Enemies) In Jail*
Led Zeppelin – Fool in the Rain (solo – Two 8ve down)
Slipknot – *Surfacing* (intro tapped bend/trill riff)
Steve Vai – *Ballerina 12/24* (two harmonies, delayed by a 1/16th and an 1/8th)
Rage Against the Machine – *Killing in the Name*
Radiohead – *My Iron Lung* (Whammy up an octave)
The White Stripes – *Ball and Biscuit*
Pink Floyd – *Marooned*

Chapter Six: Feeling the Pinch – Compression

The next two chapters feature two very different effects that are often added in the production stage of recording, but are used by guitarists in the form of compact pedals. Both compression and reverb are much subtler than other effects and are often overlooked.

Compression reduces the dynamic range of the guitar. It crushes your signal when it exceeds a set threshold, the effect of which is to make the loud parts quieter and the quiet parts louder, resulting in a more consistent sound. A loss of dynamics is normally considered a bad thing, but there are situations where some restriction is beneficial, such as the tight, spanky sound of funk guitar, for instance.

By evening out the signal response, compression adds sustain to held chords or melodies, as well as making combinations of different techniques sound more even and balanced.

A compressor has a *threshold* volume. Signal that doesn't exceed the threshold passes unaffected, while any excessively loud peaks are reduced by a controlled degree, measured by a ratio of input against output level. The waves are not clipped, as with distortion, so the general tone should be maintained.

Figure 6a shows the basic principle of compression. A repeating sequence of three different amplitude peaks is fed into a compressor. The threshold amplitude is set so that all three are affected. The shaded area is acted on by the compressor. A 2:1 ratio means everything in excess of the threshold is reduced by 50%. As the waves emerge from the compressor (on the right of the graph), you can see that the relative volumes are still present, yet proportionately smaller.

Fig. 6a

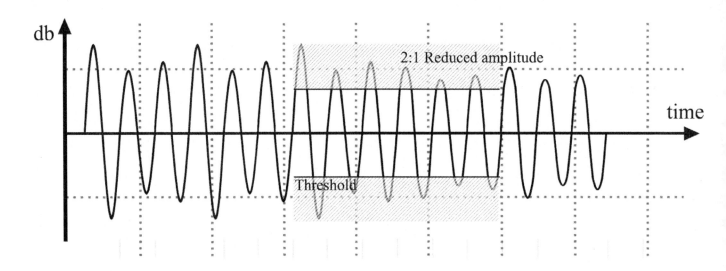

Studio rack compressors have many parameters that can fine-tune how they act upon the sound, but these are the most common controls found on the less complex guitar pedal compressors:

Sustain is a combination of threshold and ratio, and functions like an overall "compression" dial. More expensive and complex compressors will separate these out into distinct controls.

Attack controls how quickly the compressor acts upon the signal. A slower attack will allow for dynamic range, while a very fast attack will give a punchier sound to short notes.

Level adjusts the output volume. Because compressors reduce the output as they even out the dynamics, it's useful to be able to raise the affected tone so that it is comparable to the unaffected signal.

Placement in signal-chain

An unavoidable feature of compression is to raise any unwanted hum or hiss in the signal. Given that distortion pedals often introduce noise, the compressor should be placed before any gain or boost pedals. Placed early in the signal-chain it will smooth the clean guitar signal without negatively affecting the signal-to-noise balance.

The following four examples show how a compressor can add subtle polish to your tone in a variety of genres. Since compression is such a subtle effect, I've included audio with and without compression for each example.

The first example is a pop funk riff in the style of artists like Nile Rodgers and Michael Jackson. Jackson's first guitarist David Williams brought his "secret spice" to the *Off the Wall* and *Thriller* albums by providing simple motifs that are instantly memorable hooks and his influence can be heard on pop records ever since.

Funk riffs are all about being percussive, so a compressor set to a short attack can really help bring out the punchiness. There are lots of rhythmic muted notes and the compressor evens the whole part out, so these are more pronounced. Pick hard to get a bright twangy sound and use single-coil pickups if possible.

Example 6a

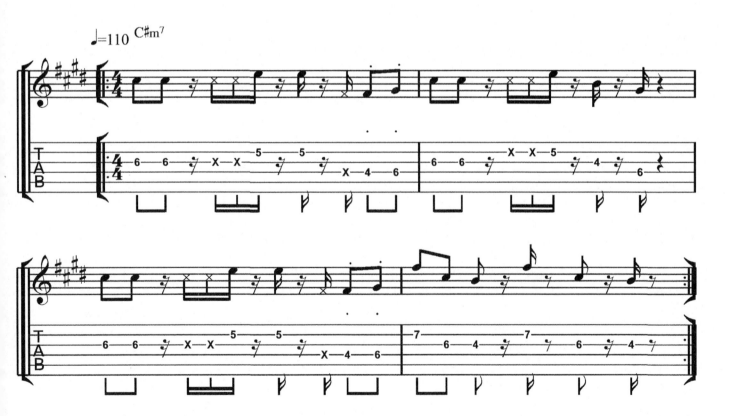

The second example uses a similar setting in a hot-country guitar phrase. The combination of pick and fingers can be dynamically inconsistent, so the compressor evens the attacks out to produce a more flowing line. Set the attack to the shortest setting to make all the attacks as machine-gun like as possible.

While the compressor can even out dynamics, it can't help with your rhythm, so take the time to get this demanding country line down slowly and accurately before shredding!

Example 6b

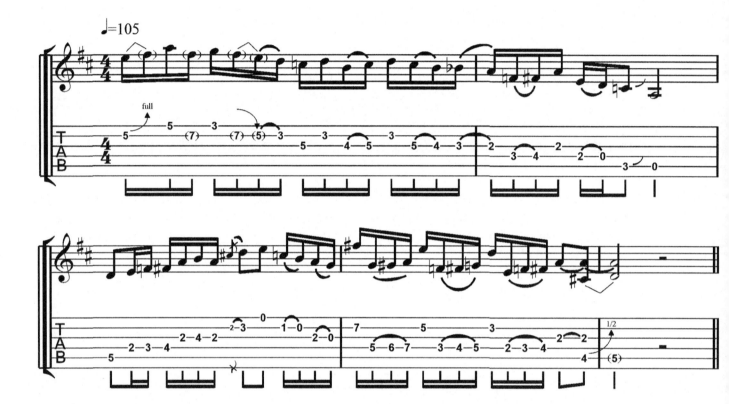

Now adding some distortion, the compressor is used to even out some tapped arpeggios. Passages that feature lots of legato, particularly hammering-on from nowhere with the fretting hand, can often be much quieter than picked notes.

The compressor makes each note sustain more as well as balancing the different string's volumes. The weaker legato notes are more dynamically balanced, giving the whole passage a smooth fluid sound.

Set the attack to moderate, a higher sustain, and high level. Switch between picking and legato and finetune the level setting until they are comparable in volume.

Example 6c

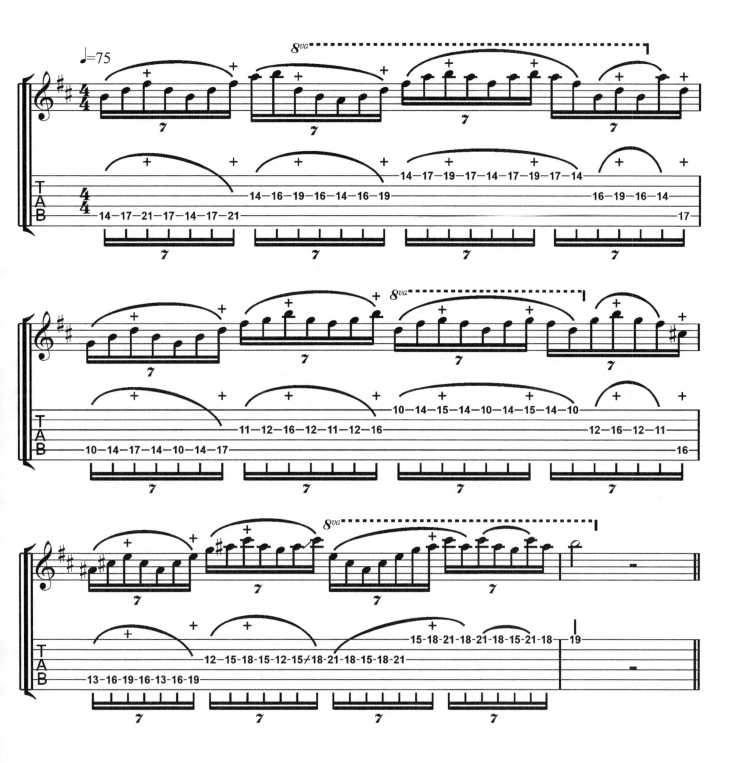

Finally, we have a percussive slap-guitar idea typical of the modern progressive metal guitarists, like Tosin Abasi of Animals as Leaders. Modern djent slap technique uses several different percussive sounds, which are sequenced to create intricate drum-like fills and rhythms. These include slapping the string with the thumb, then pushing it down through the string, hammering-on notes with the fretting hand, and slapping the flattened fretting fingers down on the strings to create dead hits.

Each of these sounds are at different volumes and a heavy compression effect will balance them all out to create a driving rhythmic sequence.

Master each of the percussive sounds in isolation until they sound clear without any compression, and start with simpler ideas such as Example 4l or classic funk basslines. The compression should be a final polish for a well-executed part.

Slaps, pops (plucking with the index or middle finger) and down/up thumb strokes are notated, all other notes are sounded by the fretting hand.

Example 6d

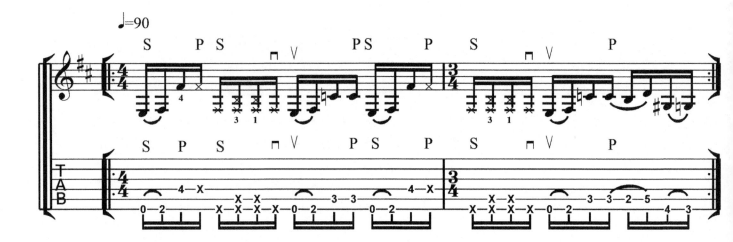

Recommended Listening for use of Compression:

Michael Jackson – *Wanna be Startin' Somethin'*
The Hellecasters – *Axe to Grind*
Daniele Gottardo - *Cardiology*
Animals as Leaders – *Infinite Regression*

Chapter Seven: Bouncing off the Walls – Reverb

Reverb is the reflection of sound round an acoustic space, so that it continues after the source has stopped. Hard surfaces reflect sound more effectively, while padded surfaces absorb and deaden the sound. *Natural reverb* is the characteristic reflections of any given space, such a cave or stone church (long reverb) or a studio or small room with soft furnishings (short reverb).

A reverb audio effect emulates these characteristics to replicate the sound of playing in such spaces where many reflections are bounced back at you one after another. This is achieved by layering many short delays. Unlike a delay pedal, each is short enough to be indistinguishable as rhythmically repeating echoes.

Reverb is another effect that is so common that its variety is often overlooked, but it adds important presence and a sense of space to a guitar tone. There are several different types of reverb, each with their own character.

Most amplifiers come with some kind of reverb built in, but having a dedicated pedal lets us control the tone much more creatively. The amp reverb is usually a spring-reverb, or a generic digital reverb being controlled by a single mix control.

Like compression, reverb is often added during production, or on the mixing desk in a gig setting. If reverb is replicating the sound of a room's sonic reflections then it is the last thing to colour the sound, and is therefore placed last in the signal path.

Also, with a dedicated reverb pedal, the effect can be placed anywhere in the signal-chain. This is of particular importance if you are using amp distortion and the effects-loop. Much like delays, reverb should usually be at the end of the chain, otherwise it will interfere with and muddy-up any distortion, pitch or modulation effects.

The most common types of reverb are:

Plate – This is the original method of artificially creating reverb. A transducer is placed on one side of a large flexible plate of sheet metal, and contact-microphones on the far side. Ripples in the plate affect the passage of signal across the plate and add a reverberant tail. This wet signal can then be mixed back in with the dry signal. Plate reverbs were used in professional studios from the late 1950s, but were large and heavy, and too delicate to be easily portable.

Spring – A similar mechanical means of creating reverb to plate. The audio is sent down a coiled wire, much like a short Slinky toy, and movements in the coil create the delayed signal. Spring reverb "tanks" are much more portable than plate reverbs, so became popular for inclusion into guitar amps.

Hall – A very long reverb, designed to emulate large reflective spaces. A large cathedral will typically have a reverb tail of about 7-10 seconds.

Gated – A studio effect used heavily in the '80s. Gated reverbs are typically large, but cut off immediately the source sound is silent. For the duration of the sound they add a presence, but don't linger afterwards. They are often used to make snare drums sound huge in a mix without cluttering the beat up with a long-lasting reverb.

In search of some of the biggest natural reverb, experimental musicians such as the late Pauline Oliveros have recorded and performed in unusual spaces such as silos, underground fuel tanks and war-time bunkers to capture reverb times lasting in excess of a minute.

The first example is a stadium-style rock guitar solo. The grandeur of this type of playing is augmented perfectly by a huge reverb.

The reverb was provided by a **Boss RV-5** digital reverb, set to "hall" with a long reverb time, medium blend and a low tone setting. Too many high frequencies in the reverb tail clutter the main guitar part and leave the tone sounding more digitised and brittle. A more mid-range EQ gives a warmer vintage-sounding reverb.

More advanced reverb effects such as the **Strymon BigSky** have an additional control labelled "pre-delay". This delays when the effect kicks in, so there is a gap between the dry sound and the start of the reverb tail. Creating this small separation can help if the result sounds muddy and incoherent.

Example 7a

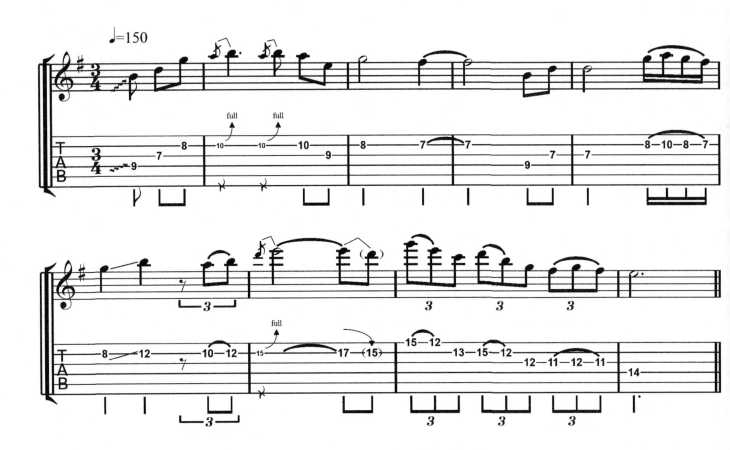

The sound of spring reverb has a characteristic oscillation within the tail, especially with louder dynamics or if the reverb tank is moved during operation. Spring reverbs are often built into guitar amps, particularly more traditional combo models, such as those made by Fender.

Spring reverb is a key ingredient to a convincing country or blues tone and especially good for surf rock. Here's a surf lick featuring a loud but short spring reverb. The reverb was provided by a 5-watt Mesa Boogie Express valve combo. At the end of the example I nudge the amp's casing to hear the springs hit against each other.

For the double-stops in bars 1-4 just dip the whammy bar gently to lower the pitch – don't worry about being exact. The chords should be hit hard at the end and muted immediately. Playing loudly will cause the spring reverb to react audibly.

Example 7b

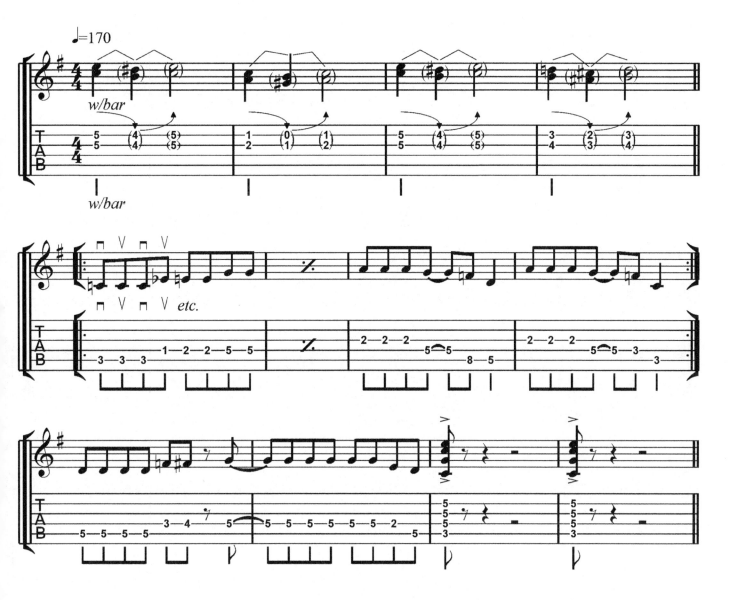

In Chapter Two, I referenced the use of gated reverb in Example 2d. This was applied to the wet signal only to give a sense of foreground and background to the dry signal and delay tails. A dry signal will make sounds appear very "close" while increasing reverb times will give the impression that sound sources are further away.

Here a similar texture is applied to funk guitar chords. The gated reverb gives the chords space and airiness, while not sacrificing their rhythmic precision and groove. Again, the **Boss RV-5** was used.

Example 7c

Finally, we have an interesting effect that is described by Anton Hunter in Chapter Nine (where I interview several guitarists about the effects they use). Contrary to the point about avoiding high-frequencies, Anton embraces them to create smooth, electronic-sounding endings to pieces.

The **Earthquaker Devices Levitation** reverb has an uncommon feature which allows high frequencies to be filtered out and fed back through the effect. Raising the feedback control causes the pedal to self-oscillate and sustain a high frequency reverb indefinitely. This is then used to blur the sound as a held chord, a loop or a delay is switched off, giving a very musical ending instead of dead stops or predictable fade-outs.

Example 7d

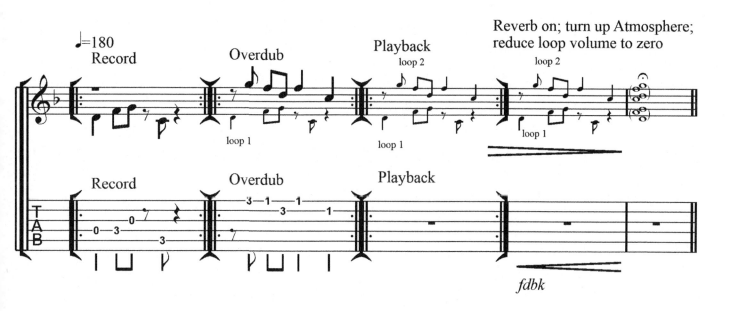

Recommended Listening for Reverb:

The Shadows – *Cavatina*
Dick Dale – *Miserlou*
Steve Vai – *For the Love of God*
The Aristocrats – *Louisville Stomp*
Sigur Rós - *Hoppípolla*

Chapter Eight: Treading the Boards – Chaining Effects and Building Pedalboards

In the previous chapters I've demonstrated the most commonly used effects, which will help you recognise when they're being used and to know when and how to employ them yourself.

However, there's a whole world of crazy effects beyond these to explore and a cottage-industry of mad scientists produce new devices all the time. Some of these are useless in actual musical situations, while others might just be revolutionary.

In this chapter I'll to move on to *chaining* effects together and examine how they interrelate. To be able to picture how the signal path will colour the sound, imagine the signal flowing through the effects in turn. Each pedal acts upon the result of the previous one, so swapping the order around can produce radically different results.

Basic Setups

It's easy for these myriad options to be overwhelming when starting out – and there are certain pedals that are more widely applicable to practical playing situations – so to start with, here is an ideal basic setup.

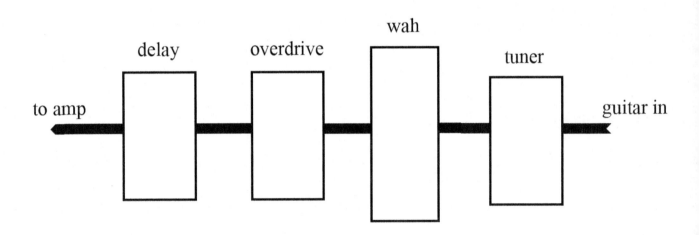

For a rock guitarist, the above combination will cover most playing situations, the primary requirement being a good-quality overdrive or distortion. The wah can provide a range of textures, the most useful of which in rock is to give a vocal expressivity to solos. The delay also enhances lead guitar parts and with a lower mix level and medium delay time can cover for reverb too.

No one wants to hear you tuning up, and asking the piano player for tuning notes mid-set looks pretty unprofessional. Whether it's a pedal or a clip-on device, a tuner is therefore essential to confidently tune, even when you can't hear properly due to poor monitoring. Set the tuner so it is silent when engaged.

Cheaper tuners are pre-set to specific tunings. Instead, look for a chromatic one as this will cater to any tuning, capo use, or other instruments.

Delay should be placed after the overdrives. If the signal enters the delay distorted, then the layers of repeats will sound like overdubs, with a clarity that doesn't mask the original. If, on the other hand, the delay provides a cloud of tails that are mixed down and run into a distortion, the signal is then "flattened" and the layers become more homogenous.

The alternative has its place, particularly if you want to highlight the process of distortion. Creating a rich texture with a delay, then slowly increasing the amount of distortion can be very effective in styles like jazz, post-rock, modern classical or electronic music.

Jazz guitarists who generally play using clean tones might be better served by looking at chorus pedals to add a depth to their tone. As we've seen, a chorus pedal can also double as a rotary speaker impersonator when set on full, ideal for blues-jazz players to enrich their accompaniment parts.

Country guitar is all about the twang, so as well as a bright-sounding guitar like a Telecaster, country players often use compressors to give each note more punch, as well as spring reverb.

Metal requires a similar setup to rock, but with more saturated distortion. More distortion brings more noise with it, making a noise-gate valuable at band volumes. Modern metal clean tones tend to be richer and more synthetic than classic rock, so dramatic reverbs and washy modulations help here.

Effects Loops

If the amp is used clean then all effects can be connected in front of the amp. If, however, you want to use effects in conjunction with the amp's distortion, then you'll need to get to grips with its effects-loop.

All guitar amps contain two discrete sections, a pre-amp and a power amp. In a nutshell: preamp = colour, power amp = power! The preamp provides the tone, distortion and EQ. The power amp will colour the sound, but its primary job is boosting the signal enough to drive the speaker.

The effects loop is a gap in the chain between these two components, into which more effects can be inserted. The preamp is essentially a distortion effect, so modulation, delay and reverb would be placed after it, in the effects loop.

As a general rule, effects that alter the signal's most basic characteristics, such as wah, compressor and distortion should be first in the chain. Effects that provide more atmospheric colouration like modulation, delay and reverb should be placed after effects that affect the tone. In short, start with the personality of the guitar, then create the sonic space in which it's being played.

All of the distorted examples in the delay and modulation chapters were recorded with effects inserted into the effects loop.

Combining Effects

To round up, I'm going to give some examples of how to combine pedals to produce more complex textures or to gain a higher degree of control over your sound.

These are just a few of my favourite combinations, so explore your own pedals to yield new and interesting results. Question the settings or sequence you've settled on in the past and see how it affects the sound.

First, I'll demonstrate how radically different a sound can be when the order of two pedals is swapped. Do you want to pitch-shift your delays or delay your pitch-shifts?

If the whammy is placed first, the delay will echo the sound of the guitar and whammy. With a long delay time this produces a studio-production-esque effect.

With the pedal order reversed, the whammy manipulates all the delay tails together.

The guitar parts couldn't be simpler, but making sharp, rhythmically accurate changes with the pedal is key to getting a smooth sound.

Example 8a (whammy – delay)

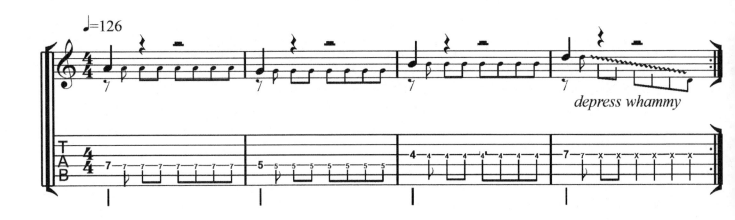

Example 8b (delay – whammy)

Another example is choosing to place a volume pedal before or after the distortion pedal. If your amp is providing the distortion, then after-distortion would mean placing it in the effects loop.

In the pre-distortion position, the volume pedal varies the signal strength that the distortion receives. If it's a good-quality overdrive this will mean the sound "cleans up" with less input volume.

Traditionally, electric guitar players "play" the amp by using the guitar's volume control, but a pedal leaves your hands free to keep playing while changing volume.

One modern player who operates is this way is Guthrie Govan, who uses a volume pedal in the pre-distortion position. His amp is set to be quite saturated with overdrive, and cleaner tones are produced by backing off the volume pedal.

On the other hand, to replicate that classic *Don't Stop Believing* lick, the volume pedal is placed AFTER the dirt. This allows the tone to be fully distorted throughout while fading in from nothing.

The Journey fade-in was most-likely added at the mixing stage for the studio recording, but this method gives the same effect in a live setting.

The second example features a thrash metal riff fading in slowly and ominously, as if from a distance. If the sound was clean and weak-sounding to start with, it would lose all its ferocious impact.

Example 8c (vol. pedal - overdrive)

Example 8d (overdrive – vol. pedal)

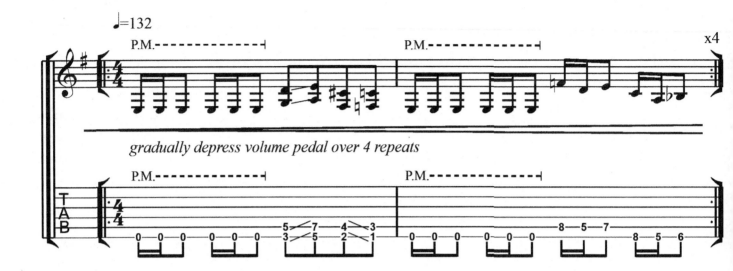

The next example splits the signal into a wet (effected) and dry (direct) path, so the effect can be mixed in and out while playing. There are pedals that split and mix the two back together again before the amp, such as the **Boss Line Selector**. In this instance, I'm using a **Boss DD-7 Digital Delay**, sending wet and dry to a two-amp setup.

Steve Morse (Deep Purple/Dixie Dregs) uses this trick to fade the delay in and out. A long delay adds space to melodic playing, but held bends often make faster licks sound messy and incoherent.

In this solo excerpt I use the volume pedal to fade out the delay part during the busier moments and bring it back in afterwards.

The same concept could be used with other effects such as phaser or tremolo. It does the same job as the mix/level pot found on most pedals, but by *side-chaining* the pedal you can alter the balance while still playing.

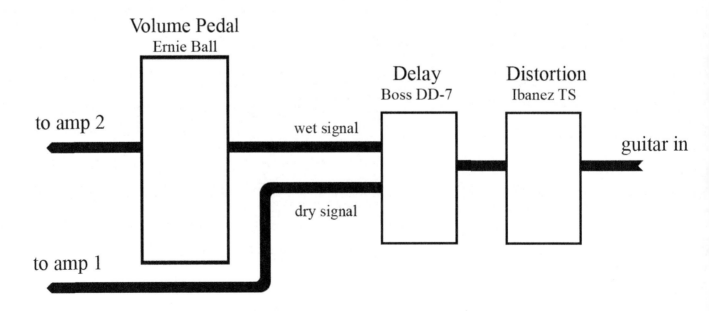

Example 8e

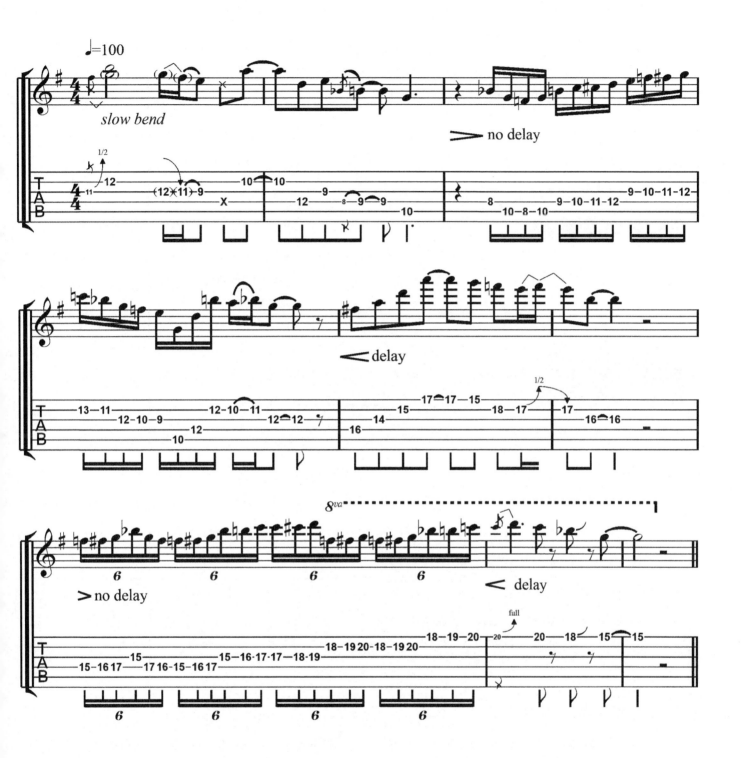

Multiple distortions can be chained together to produce a tone that shares each pedal's characteristics. As I said in Chapter One, combining several pedals, each contributing a small amount of gain, produces a much more focused sound that delivers punch while retaining clarity.

The following example features three-note chords in a progressive metal riff which would sound very mushy through one pedal or an amp turned up high. The compressor squashes the volume of the chords to balance the quieter single note line at the end.

This setup featured no less than six gain stages, but the benefits are still very noticeable with two stages, which could be two overdrive pedals, or a pedal and amp distortion. As with Example 6e, the signal was split after the compressor.

The left channel ran through an **Ibanez Tubescreamer** and **Wampler Dual Fusion** (set to the vintage voicing) into a Mesa Boogie Dual Rectifier. The right channel used a **Big Muff** into a **Reaper Pandemonium** into a Randall V2 head. The gain on each was set between 1-5.

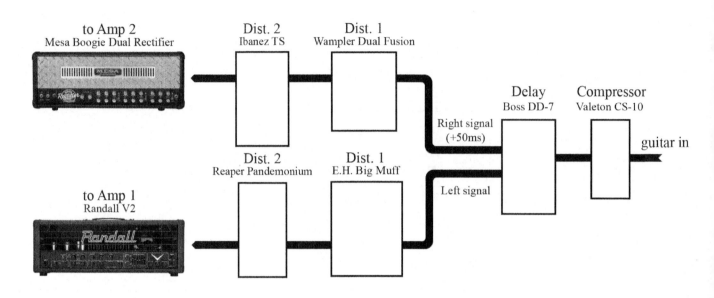

Example 8f

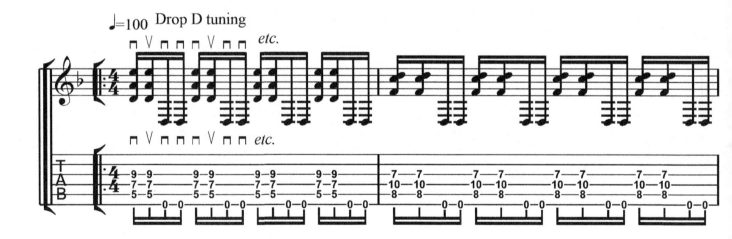

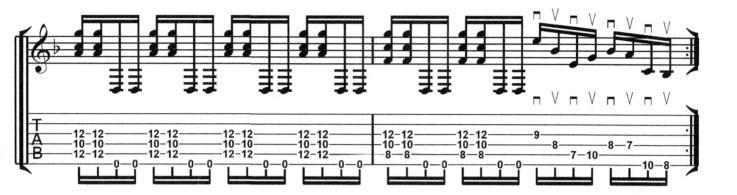

We end the book with an ethereal soundscape which doesn't sound like a guitar at all! I'm employing two delays (**EH Memory Boy Deluxe**, and **Boss DD-7**) the **KMA Moai Maea** octave pedal and **KMA Astrospurt** phaser.

Example 8g

Here's the signal path:

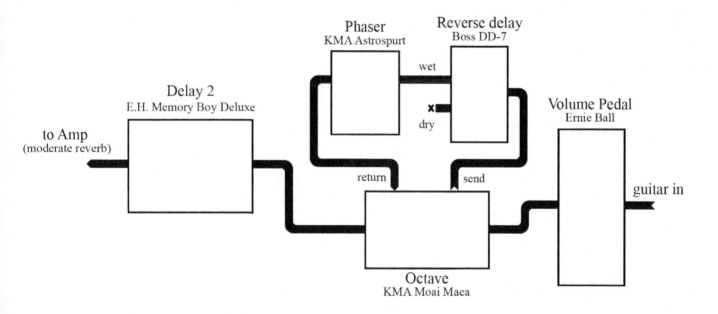

The Moai Maea's effects loop is the at core of this sound. The clean guitar signal is sent to the loop, but the pitch-shifted octaves are untouched. This feature stops the lower tones getting muddy, which is easily done, especially with lots of delay.

The clean guitar is then treated to a reverse delay and the original signal removed. The reversed delay tails are then sent to the phaser for added colour before returning to the effects loop and being mixed back in with the sub-octave.

The whole sound is then delayed again by the Memory Boy. This is just a medium length delay to smooth out any rough edges. The Moai Maea is monophonic and will only accept single notes, so the second delay gives a bit of a polyphonic texture to the end result, just like rubbing a pastel drawing to blur the distinct lines together.

To complete the sound, I used an Ebow and volume pedal to give each note a very slow attack. The result is a rich and atmospheric pad-like synth sound. It's no surprise that post-rock bands such as Mogwai use such extensive effects setups.

The recording features a short improvisation in the Aeolian mode, using very long notes to let the effects do the talking.

Chapter Nine: What Pedals Are You Using?

To close the book, I talk to three very different guitarists on their individual approaches to tone and equipment. These conversations show that there as many different paths to take with guitar effects as there are players. There is no substitute for experimenting with gear and exploring new options in the search for the sonic holy grail.

www.antonhunter.com / @hunteranton

Anton Hunter

First, we meet Manchester-based improvising guitarist Anton Hunter, guitarist for internationally touring Beats & Pieces Big Band, Sloth Racket and Article XI, as well as a host of other ad-hoc improvised groups.

You're usually referred to as a "jazz" guitarist, so people might be surprised to see you use this setup if they haven't heard your playing. Are there any guitarists who inspired you to go down this route?

I've always been into pedals and changing the sound of the guitar. When I was a youth that would have been bands like Radiohead & Mogwai, especially Jonny Greenwood, who get these huge walls of noise. It's interesting delays and making a guitar sound like "not a guitar". I was quite into Mick McCave from The Verve. Before *Urban Hymns* they were a four piece, *A Northern Soul*, and the album before [*No Come Down*] was delay-laden, so I got into delay pedals a lot.

In terms of people who would be identifiable as "jazz" guitarists, seeing local hero Stuart McCallum live when I was first getting into jazz was like "Oh, you CAN combine effects and jazz language or approaches." Then Bill Frisell and Nels Cline, who both have a pedal collection that would put mine to shame. Yet, Bill still sounds like himself whether on an acoustic guitar or using loads of loops and delays, freeze pedals and whatever, distortion, same with Nels Cline.

How did you arrive at your current extensive effects setup?

Gradually is the one-word answer. It's evolved over a long time. I can't remember when I got a flight-case and stuck things down, but for a long time I carried around a sports bag and set them all up each gig. I'd do it in basically the conventional order, so pitch [shifting], distortion, then delay, roughly.

A while back I moved the volume pedal to after all the dirt, so you can get this: [plays a faded-in saturated distortion chord]. So it's already incredibly fuzzy before it starts fading in.

When I bought the **Earthquaker Devices Levitation** [reverb] everything had to make way and I realised I wasn't using the tremolo, so that went. It's in a constant state of evolution, I guess.

You manipulate effect settings in real-time a lot while playing. Do you have a way of consciously practising this in a creative or technical way?

Definitely in a creative way. So, I'll do what might be described as a solo ambient improvisation, with a loop pedal and delays. I hear this stuff when I'm improvising: "Oh, I want such and such," or "I can hear this coming in" then I try to make it happen.

I'm not really a good user of the loop pedal rhythmically, partly because this **Ditto** is a one-button pedal so there's no separate stop button. That is something that I should practise from a technical standpoint.

Do you use any of the pedals in particularly unorthodox ways?

A lot of people would put the loop last in the signal chain – the idea being that you've got a sound and you want to loop it, so it goes last, especially if you're building up layers into a composition.

Instead, I mostly use it for texture, but if I do use it for a repeating pattern, then I've got a flanger, delay and a reverb after it. That means each loop will be different if, for example, the flanger repeats on a different time period. It stops the ear getting bored by the repetition. That's something about people using loops to build up compositions, it gets really boring because it's just the same four bars round and round again. This is a way of acknowledging that and being able to change how the loop sounds without starting and stopping it.

The **Levitation Reverb** from Earthquaker Devices has an "atmosphere" control which feeds the high frequencies back through the pedal again. Because the pedals are after the loop, I can stick the repeats right up, so it goes into self-oscillation, and you've got a really sophisticated fadeout, compared to just turning the loop pedal's volume down, or stopping it dead.

The **Saturn Works Feedback Looper** is an effects loop for the whole pedalboard with a bypass and volume out. The other side is a momentary feedback looper that controls the amount of sound that goes back round into the start of the board. So, the Feedback Looper is able to turn off a big wall of noise, but also create it, which is really impractical and none of your readers will want to do this!

Read the full interview with Anton Hunter online https://www.fundamental-changes.com/exploring-guitar-effects-interviews

Anton's Rig:

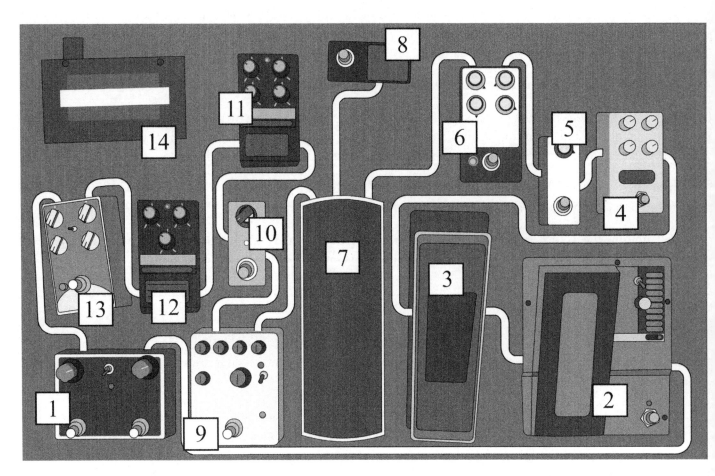

1 Saturn Works Feedback Looper	**8 TC Electronic** Polytune
2 Digitech Whammy V	**9 Red Panda** Particle
3 Vox Wah	**10 TC Electronic** Ditto
4 Empress Germ Drive	**11 Loco Box** Flanger
5 Z-Vex Super Hard-On (clone)	**12 Loco Box** Analog Delay
6 Earthquaker Devices Terminal	**13 Earthquaker Devices** Levitation
7 Ernie Ball Volume	**14 Voodoo Lab** Pedal power 2 (power supply)

Nik Svarc

Next up is Leeds-based guitarist and educator Nik Svarc. Nik regularly performs around the country with his jazz-rock trio as well as with a host of noted jazz musicians.

www.niksvarc.com / @niksvarc

Were there any particular guitarists or songs that inspired your tone and use of effects?

Later on, it was John Scofield for mixing blues and jazz, as well as his use of modulation. Wayne Krantz, for his use of the wah and MoogerFooger. Bill Frisell too – the amount of variety in his playing – jazz, country, Americana, rock – is amazing. Holdsworth was another big influence. Secrets was an amazing album. I never got into the midi-guitar thing live, but I use one for composing at home. Wayne Krantz uses effects in interesting ways, like putting the wah in front of the MoogerFooger (ring modulator) so the wah shifts the affected frequency range. He also uses an old DD-3 just because it sounds a bit crummy compared to a modern studio 24-bit delay like a Timeline. So, I learnt a lot by listening and watching him play and being that geek who goes up to the stage to look at the pedalboard.

How did you arrive at your current setup?

I don't just play crazy jazz, I have to play lots of different types of gigs. It took a long time to build that board up. Basically, I wanted a workable board I can use for any gig. So, I just add things around that for different gigs, rather than having two boards. I'd use most of it on a function gig, maybe apart from the Freeze pedal.

I just have the standard things. Three different types of distortion: The Wampler Tumnus, an old modded Ibanez 808 Tubescreamer and a Pro Co Rat. The Tumnus sounds amazing when stacked with other distortions, but sometimes that's too noisy at stage volumes. Then there's an old Rat. I'm obsessed with Rat pedals, I've got about four, but that's a mid-80s one and seems to sound warmest. The chorus is an old Boss CE-2. There's nothing on the board that's too expensive or difficult to replace.

The **MF-102** ring modulator makes all those Dalek sounds, but it's an interesting pedal because you can also use it as a tremolo. It makes a really nice tremolo. You hear it in Krantz's music. There's a whole range from Moog that look the same, but do different things. There's a very nice analogue delay pedal but it's really expensive.

I used to have a digital ring modulator; I didn't like it at all. Some effects I don't like to be digital, while others can sound cool. I really don't like digital chorus; old analogue chorus just sounds so much different. I use chorus in a different way. There's a trick I stole off Schofield: turn every setting up to create a Lesley [rotary speaker] sound, and it only works with an analogue chorus. If you do it with a digital chorus it just sounds terrible. Digital delays are great though, because you can tap-tempo them. Analogue delays are not always so precise.

Amp-wise, I use a Fender Twin, Mesa Boogie Lonestar or Vox AC-15. There's quite a wide range of sounds available from those amps. I occasionally use the drive channels, but usually just run them on clean or get the AC-15 to just break up.

I see you've got three different delays. How do they work together – or are they just different settings?

I love the **Line6 DL-4**. I know it's old, but when it came out it was the only thing that could do that many things. Now you can buy a Timeline or whatever, and they'd sound better, but I still love it, mainly for the loop sampler. I use that quite a lot for creating soundscapes and so forth.

The **Boss DD-6** has a function called Warp, which captures a note or chord in a really bizarre, stuttering kind of way. It's similar to the Freeze, and I used it before the Freeze came out. I only use that pedal for the warp function. Marc Ducret [*avantgarde* improvising/jazz guitarist] uses that sound, also Chris Sharkey from Trio VD and metal bands like Dillinger Escape Plan.

The **DD-3** just has a classic delay that sounds great to my ears. I've always liked it. I use that for quite long delays, a lot of volume swells and creating ambience. So, each one just has its different vibe really.

How would you practise integrating effects into your general playing vocabulary?

Use effects as part of your practice, rather than seeing them as a separate thing to your instrument. See it all as one thing for creating a sound. I think a lot of people don't practise with their effects. I know a lot of my students don't. They turn up to a gig and expect it to work, but it doesn't work like that – you've got to figure out what settings you want to use. I like to have everything sorted out before I even enter a rehearsal.

Read the full interview with Nik online at https://www.fundamental-changes.com/exploring-guitar-effects-interviews

Nik's Rig:

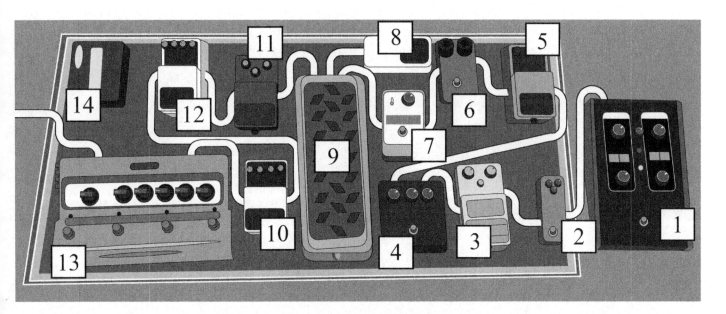

1 MoogerFooger Ring Modulator	**8 Volume Pedal**
2 Wampler Tumnus	**9 TC Electronic** Polytune
3 Ibanez Tubescreamer	**10 Boss** Octave OC-2
4 Pro Co. Rat	**11 Boss** DD-3 Digital Delay
5 Boss CE-3 Chorus	**12 Boss** DD-6 Digital Delay
6 MXR Dyna Comp	**13 Line 6** DL-4 Delay Modeller
7 Electro Harmonix Freeze	**14 T-Rex** Fuel Tank (power supply)

Richard Shaw

Finally, I talk to the multi-faceted Richard Shaw, guitarist for veteran UK extreme metal band Cradle of Filth, who also maintains plenty of teaching and musical theatre gigs.

www.cradleoffilth.com / @richardshawguitarist

Could you outline the rig you're using for Cradle of Filth, for the tours and recording?

Okay, so recording and touring are two completely different rigs. Live we're using Mooer products at the moment.

Weirdly enough, Ashok [Marek "Ashok" Smerda, other Cradle guitarist] and I both stumbled across the Mooer preamps that came out around a year ago, and bought the one based on the **EVH 5150 III**. They're so small they don't even fit a battery in them. I thought, "Oh my God, these are incredible!" They sound great DI'd and now we use the **Mooer Radar** cab simulator too. So, we go from the preamp into the cab simulator, all in two pedals!

Firstly, we go into a **Shure GL XD** wireless unit, which is also a tuner, so that takes the tuner out the equation, into the Mooer preamp and cab emulator, then that goes straight into the mixing desk and everything goes into the in-ear mix, so everything's kind of controlled for us by the monitor engineer. It's just one high-gain tone that stays on for the whole night, which we get from that Mooer preamp, and even when we do a solo, our front-of-house sound guy will boost it and put a bit of delay on it.

Around 18 months ago we were using **Kempers** [high-end profiling amp-modeller] but they belong to our old tour manager, and when he went off with a bigger band, he took them with him. They're very practical and sound great, but for Cradle of Filth, it's about £1500 for one tone.

We moved to Mooers partly because my entire rig could fit in my guitar case, which is brilliant because flights, oversize baggage and extra luggage all cost money, and if you're flying every day that adds up.

Mooer have been really supportive too. Once they'd cottoned onto the fact that we were using them, they sent us a couple of free ones for backups and to try out the latest models.

In the studio it's a different story. We use heads and cabs and try out all kinds of effects and acoustic guitars. PRS, whose guitars I use, sent me an amp that they'd been working on, the **PRS Archon**, and they just wanted to know what I thought about it. We ended up using the Archon on pretty much all the rhythm tones and all of my lead tones on the last album [*Cryptoniana – The Seductiveness of Decay*]. I think the speaker cabinet was a Mesa Boogie 4x12.

For my side of the rhythm tones, because we were double tracking, I used the PRS Archon and then Scott re-amped the same take with an original **Peavey 5150**. The 5150 is the go-to metal amp for good reason – they're so good at blending. The PRS, blended with the 5150, creates this huge tone, just from one guitar part.

The Archon is one of the clearest distorted tones I've heard. When you play a chord, you can hear every single individual note in that chord. The 5150 has that low end and low-mid punch that gets you in your chest when you palm-mute.

You've done a lot of theatre work, which is about variety and matching so many requirements. How would you prepare for that?

Sometimes you're lucky enough that the score tells you what kind of sound is wanted, especially for the rockier ones – *We Will Rock You, Rock of Ages, Jesus Christ Superstar* etc. They do say what tone you need. More traditional scores won't and you've got to piece it together. You should go through this with the musical director at the first rehearsal, or prior to it, and ask what he would like, or get some recordings of the show. It's just doing my homework really. I'll make notes of what's needed and assemble a pedalboard from there.

Over the years I've accumulated loads of amps and effects pedals, so, when it comes to cover gigs and musical theatre, I assemble a purpose-built pedalboard for that show. I'll take out all the unnecessary stuff, just in case anything happens during a show; I'll take the bare minimum setup. The thing about musical theatre is there's not much room in an orchestra pit, so you want all the tones in the smallest space. There's no room for a great big pedalboard. Instead of having an acoustic guitar that'll take up room on a stand, I'll usually have an acoustic simulator. It depends how prominent the acoustic part is, but a simulator does a good enough job if it's just here and there.

The number one rule is that it's all got to be super-quiet. When it's in bypass it's got to be silent. Any hum would go through the front-of-house, and you don't want anything disrupting the dialogue.

I'd research getting the quietest overdrive pedals to avoid hum. Actually, the Mooer stuff is really good for that as well. I've been using Mooer stuff for years for theatre and it has worked really well.

I'm thinking of speaking to Line6 and upgrading to a **Helix**. I think they're the way forward, since you can programme everything for each situation and not have to swap pedals in and out. For me, it's a really exciting time for digital technology because it's almost caught up with analogue. I wouldn't say it's quite there – I still prefer the sound of amps and cabs, and real speakers pushing air – but it's scary how close it's got. Once upon a time I wouldn't have thought of using the little Mooer preamp for Cradle of Filth, not in a million years, but it is really convincing.

Have you used multi-fx in the past, or have you always been into traditional compact pedals?

I've usually been that kind of guy to be honest, with the separate pedals. I like the tone and feel of them, even the good-old Boss pedals. People slag them off once they get to a certain level and go for "boutique amps" but I think some Boss pedals are still great. There's a reason why Zakk Wylde had an **SD-1** in his rig for so many years. They're underrated pedals, and affordable.

I lean towards individual stomp-boxes, but have a **Line 6 M5**. I'll have all my usual pedals – the wah, overdrives, a couple of modulations – but then there's always some parts in a show where I need an odd tone for one song, that I'll use for 10 seconds in the whole set, like for example a Lesley [rotary] cabinet emulator or something.

I looked at the individual Lesley cabinet emulator and it's about 400 quid [£], and the M5 was about 90 quid. Line6 get a bad rap, but to my ears it sounded better!

I think tone is a combination of everything. It's very difficult just to say, "Buy this" and "buy that" and you'll sound like this. I remember trying an exact replica of Brian May's rig and was very disappointed to find I sounded like me. I even used a sixpence to play and everything!

That was the moment I realized it's not a bad thing, actually it's a good thing, because it doesn't matter what I play through, I'll sound like me. Finding the magical combination of guitar, pickups, pick, amp and pedals gets that extra 10% that makes your tone, but I'm still a big believer that 90% of your tone comes from your fingers.

Read the full interview with Richard online: https://www.fundamental-changes.com/exploring-guitar-effects-interviews

Appendix:
A Little Physics for the Curious

To clarify how each effect works and the differences between them, let's roll up our sleeves and delve into a bit of science.

Understanding how sound waves behave underpins synthesis, acoustics, recording techniques and, of course, controlling effects. The following concepts are widely applicable to music in general and worth getting a basic familiarity with.

I've simplified the models and kept them relevant to our application, but they provide a functional introduction to much of audio physics known as *acoustics*.

Overtones

Though you might think you're just playing an open A string (110hz) in fact there a multitude of higher frequencies (*overtones*) that also resonate in sympathy with that A (the *fundamental*). These harmonic overtones combine with the fundamental to produce a more complex compound waveform.

The relative volume of each harmonic is what makes the same note sound different on each instrument. Fig. 8a shows a fundamental wave, for example 110Hz.

Fig. 8a

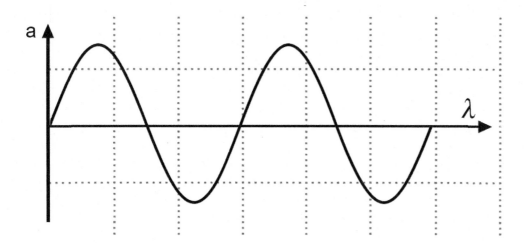

The first harmonic that would resonate with it is an octave above, with a frequency of 220hz, which has half the fundamental.

Fig. 8b

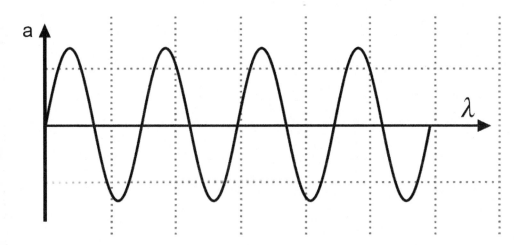

When two waves occur simultaneously their amplitudes are summed together to produce a single, more complex waveform.

Fig. 8c

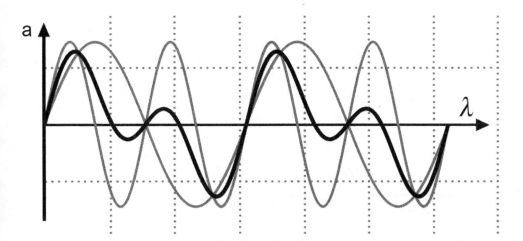

It is because even one note has a whole spectrum of frequencies within the signal, that these component frequencies can be isolated and manipulated with effects like modulation, EQ and wah-wah/filters.

Clipping and Distortion

Overdrive is also referred to as "clipping", usually when it is unwanted, as in recording situations. Clipping describes what is actually happening to the soundwave. When the amplitude gets too wide for the equipment to carry, the signal becomes restricted and "squared off".

Fig. 8d Waveform clipping

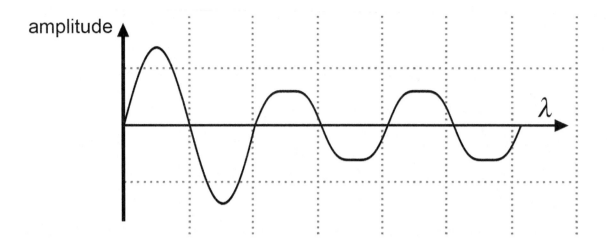

The resulting square-edged wave introduces lots of higher harmonics (see Fig. 8b) to the original signal. This because it is the sum of all simultaneous waves that together produce the overall waveform.

Notice that the overall amplitude is narrower (quieter) below than the initial sine wave and layering additional waves on top. This explains why distortion compresses the sound and needs to be turned up more than a clean signal to cut through.

Fig. 8e *Fourier Analysis*

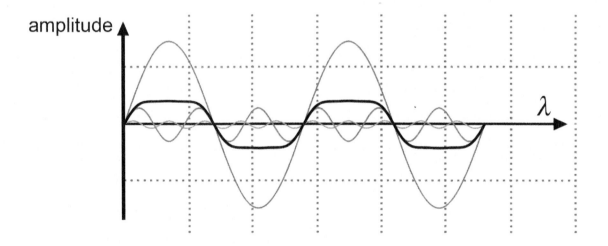

Phase Cancellation

Remember the summing together of simultaneous component waveforms that produced the square waves from distortion? Well, the same behaviour occurs when two identical waves are played *out of phase*. The *phase* of a wave refers to its point in the cycle. Phase is measured in degrees, so the start of the wave is 0° and the point where it crosses back over the centre at halfway is 180°.

Fig. 8f shows two sine waves. The darker wave is 90° behind the grey one. It crosses the centre line at 90°, or a quarter of a cycle later.

Fig. 8f

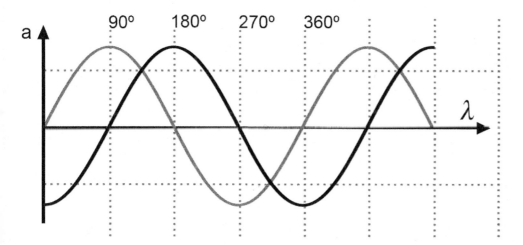

The result of two soundwaves heard out of phase is a destructive combination, and a noticeable dip in volume or a "hollow" tone. If the two waves are exactly 180° apart, they cancel each other out exactly, resulting in silence.

The following three graphs illustrate this phenomenon by showing the same wave at different out of phase positions. Notice how the combined wave decreases in amplitude (volume) as it approaches 180° out of phase.

Fig. 8g – 90° phase difference

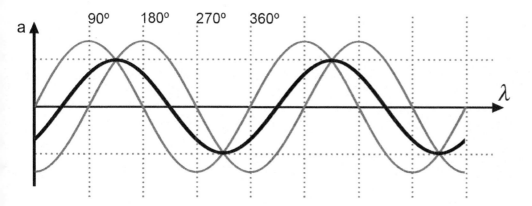

Fig. 8h – 135° phase difference

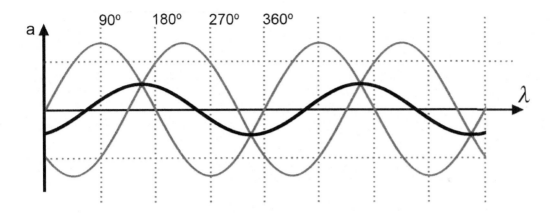

Fig. 8i – 180° phase difference

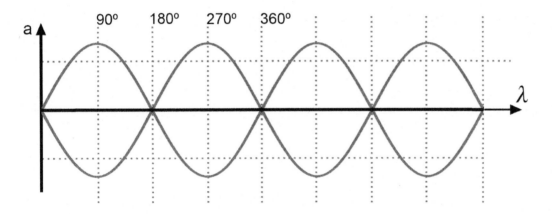

Low Frequency Oscillators (LFOs)

Low-frequency oscillators are common electrical components in synthesizers and modulation effects. The LFO is a tone generator just like that found in any synth, but detuned so the wave's oscillation is so slow it's below the range of human hearing.

The continuously changing amplitude of the wave is then used to automatically control an external effect.

Figure 8j illustrates how a wave would correspond to an adjustable level control. As the wave travels through its cycle, the rotary knob underneath moves accordingly. Here the amplitude has been given a scale of +5 to -5, which translate to 0 to 10 on the effect parameter.

Fig. 8j

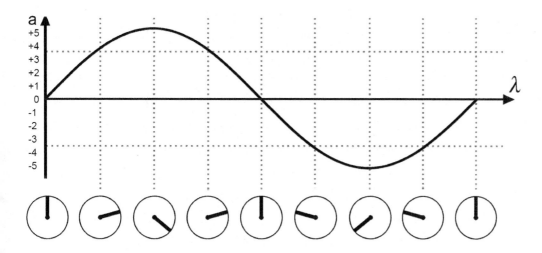

A typical use is to assign an LFO to control the rate and shape of a tremolo effect. The wave dictates the rise and fall in output volume.

Figure 8k would give a subtle pulsating tremolo, while figure 8l's steeper sided square wave would give an on/off stuttering effect.

Fig. 8k

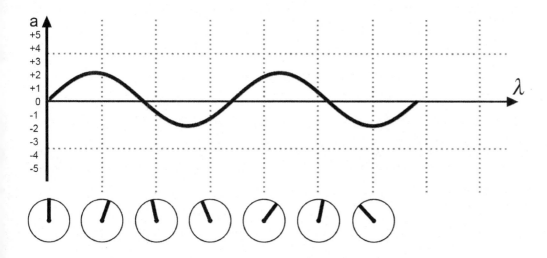

Fig. 81

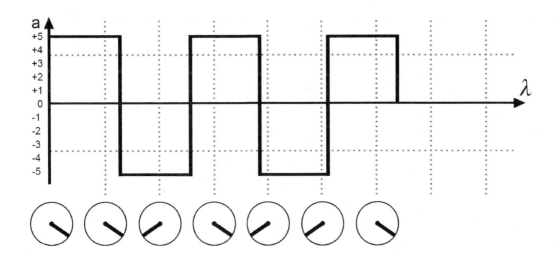

While not at all essential to be a great guitarist, having an awareness of these principles will benefit you in several important respects – such as being able to find solutions to technical problems more easily and being able to picture the way effects will colour the sound before hearing. This is especially useful for trying to create sounds you've first heard in your head, or to replicate non-guitar sounds.

Have fun!

Other Books from Fundamental Changes

The Complete Guide to Playing Blues Guitar Book One: Rhythm Guitar

The Complete Guide to Playing Blues Guitar Book Two: Melodic Phrasing

The Complete Guide to Playing Blues Guitar Book Three: Beyond Pentatonics

The Complete Guide to Playing Blues Guitar Compilation

The CAGED System and 100 Licks for Blues Guitar

Minor ii V Mastery for Jazz Guitar

Jazz Blues Soloing for Guitar

Guitar Scales in Context

Guitar Chords in Context

The First 100 Chords for Guitar

Jazz Guitar Chord Mastery

Complete Technique for Modern Guitar

Funk Guitar Mastery

The Complete Technique, Theory & Scales Compilation for Guitar

Sight Reading Mastery for Guitar

Rock Guitar Un-CAGED

The Practical Guide to Modern Music Theory for Guitarists

Beginner's Guitar Lessons: The Essential Guide

Chord Tone Soloing for Jazz Guitar

Chord Tone Soloing for Bass Guitar

Voice Leading Jazz Guitar

Guitar Fretboard Fluency

The Circle of Fifths for Guitarists

First Chord Progressions for Guitar

The First 100 Jazz Chords for Guitar

100 Country Licks for Guitar

Pop & Rock Ukulele Strumming

Walking Bass for Jazz and Blues

Guitar Finger Gym

The Melodic Minor Cookbook

The Chicago Blues Guitar Method

Heavy Metal Rhythm Guitar

Heavy Metal Lead Guitar

Progressive Metal Guitar

Heavy Metal Guitar Bible

Exotic Pentatonic Soloing for Guitar

The Complete Jazz Guitar Soloing Compilation

The Jazz Guitar Chords Compilation

Fingerstyle Blues Guitar

The Complete DADGAD Guitar Method

Country Guitar for Beginners

Beginner Lead Guitar Method

The Country Fingerstyle Guitar Method

Beyond Rhythm Guitar

Rock Rhythm Guitar Playing

Fundamental Changes in Jazz Guitar

Neo-Classical Speed Strategies for Guitar

100 Classic Rock Licks for Guitar

The Beginner's Guitar Method Compilation

100 Classic Blues Licks for Guitar

The Country Guitar Method Compilation

Country Guitar Soloing Techniques

Printed in Great Britain
by Amazon

21681461R00066